Raising an Aging Parent

"*Raising an Aging Parent* provides an empowering roadmap for turning the many changes and challenges we will face as our parents age, into new opportunities to find peace, love and healing in our families."
—DANIEL BURRUS, New York Times bestselling author of seven books including *Flash Foresight: How to See the Invisible and Do the Impossible*

"SO potent and such perfect timing! *Raising an Aging Parent* is a must-read for all of us who are navigating the changes and challenges of aging parents, particularly if you also have children. Written with understanding, compassion and practical wisdom, Ken Druck provides a clear course for finding peace with our parents, siblings and ourselves, as we navigate the decisions ahead. I found myself shedding a tear more than once, laughing out loud and nodding in firm agreement throughout this book."
—MARI SMITH, Social Media Thought Leader and author, *The New Relationship Marketing*

"Every aging child, and every aging parent should read this book by Dr. Ken Druck. This "how to" book prepares you for caring for your parent and yourself whatever your age."
—DEBORAH SZEKELY, age ninety-seven, Founder of The Golden Door and Huffington Post's "Godmother of Wellness"

"With two aging parents in their eighties this could not have come at a better time for me and my siblings. This book is a brilliant guidebook for helping us find peace with ourselves and our parents."

—JOHN ASSARAF, New York Times bestselling author, *The Answer,* and Chairman/CEO, Neurogym

"Whether this reality has arrived in your life suddenly, or gradually . . . or is simply something you recognize the need to prepare for . . . you will find in these pages a roadmap for navigating your emotions, your parents' emotions, and the day-to-day complexities of transitioning from being a child—to parenting your own parent."

—RAMANANDA JOHN E. WELSHONS, author, *When Prayers Aren't Answered*

"This family-empowering bible provides a clear action plan for resolving conflict, strengthening communication, and bringing out the best in your family and yourself during the most difficult of times so you can celebrate the best of times—together. Read it before you need it!"

—MARY MARCDANTE, author, *My Mother, My Friend;* Contributing author, *Chicken Soup for the Mother's Soul*

"*Raising an Aging Parent* is a very good book by a very good man. Ken Druck brings forth grace and kindness wherever he goes. This book covers every aspect of being a family including diffusing sibling rivalries, opening doors of communication, and moving forward after a parent dies. We have found peace and comfort in these pages."

—STEWART EMERY, coauthor, international best sellers, *Success Built to Last, Do You Matter,* and *Who's In Your Room*

"I am struck by the depth and breadth with which Ken Druck covers a very complex subject. Reliving the challenges of helping midwife my Mom's death and watching my partner slip into vascular dementia this past year, I am finding a newfound peace in these pages."

—BARBARA BROWN, Ph.D., Clinical Psychologist

Raising an Aging
PARENT

Other Books by Ken Druck

Courageous Aging: Your Best Years Ever Reimagined

*The Real Rules of Life:
Balancing Life's Terms with Your Own*

How to Talk to Your Kids About School Violence

The Secrets Men Keep - Breaking the Silence Barrier

Audio Books

Courageous Aging: Your Best Years Ever Reimagined

Healing Your Life After the Loss of a Loved One

Booklets

The Handbook for Self-Care

Psychological Estate Planning (with Tony Silvia, Esq.)

The Do's and Don'ts of Grief Support

Raising an Aging
PARENT

*Guidelines for Families in the
Second Half of Life*

Dr. Ken Druck

Redwood Publishing, LLC

Copyright © 2019 by Ken Druck

All rights reserved. No part of this publication may be reproduced, distributed, or transmitted in any form or by any means, including photocopying, recording, or other electronic or mechanical methods, without the prior written permission of the publisher, except in the case of brief quotations embodied in critical reviews and certain other noncommercial uses permitted by copyright law. For permission requests, write to the publisher, addressed "Attention: Permissions Coordinator," at info@redwoodigitalpublishing.com

Printed in the United States of America
First Printing, 2019

Published by Redwood Publishing, LLC (Ladera Ranch, California)
www.redwooddigitalpublishing.com

Disclaimer: Although the author and publisher have made every effort to ensure that the information in this book was correct at press time, the author and publisher do not assume and hereby disclaim any liability to any party for any loss, damage, or disruption caused by errors or omissions, whether such errors or omissions result from negligence, accident, or any other cause. Separately, this book is designed to provide information and motivation to its readers. It is sold with the understanding that the author and publisher are not engaged to render any type of psychological, legal, or any other kind of professional advice. The content of each article is the sole expression and opinion of its author and is not meant to substitute for any advice from your healthcare professionals, lawyers, therapists, business advisors/partners, or personal connections.

ISBN 978-1-947341-80-7 (hardcover)
ISBN 978-1-947341-81-4 (paperback)
ISBN 978-1-947341-82-1 (e-book)

Library of Congress Cataloguing Number: 2019915391

Book Design by Redwood Publishing, LLC
    - Cover Design: Michelle Manley
    - Interior Design: Ghislain Viau
    - Cover photography: Images by Lisette – Lisette Omoss

10 9 8 7 6 5 4 3 2 1

*To my beloved grandsons, Stone and Andrix,
who will have started raising their mother, Stefie,
and father, Tony, many years before they're able to read
their names inscribed in this book.*

*My love will be with "the Four Silvias"
forever and always.*

Table of Contents

Foreword xiii

Author's Note xvii

Introduction 1

Chapter 1: There's Nothing Easy About Watching Your Parents Get Older. 5

Chapter 2: Family Role Reversal: Are You Becoming the Parent? 23

Chapter 3: What Your Parents Would Tell You, if Only They Could 43

Chapter 4: Caregiving Is a Two-Way Street. 59

Chapter 5: "I'll Never Give Up My Car Keys!"— When Parents Resist Change 73

Chapter 6: "Mom Always Liked You Best!"— When Sibling Rivalries Resurface. 91

Chapter 7: Rising to the Occasion: The Sandwich Generation 105

Chapter 8: How Much Is Enough: The Real Responsibilities of Adult Children 117

Chapter 9: Making the Tough Calls: Where They Live, What They Spend, What Medical Care They May Need 133

Chapter 10: Living Losses: Diminishment, Dementia, Dishonor 149

Chapter 11: The Infinite Finality of Death 163

Chapter 12: Managing Your Own Needs in the Second Half of Life 183

Chapter 13: Leaving a Legacy of Love: Creating the Best Possible Future 201

Foreword

When Dr. Ken Druck shared *Raising an Aging Parent* with me, I got goosebumps. It was almost as if he had been eavesdropping on my life for the last three years. My path to assuming my current role as President of the Oasis Institute, a national non-profit with a broad focus on successful aging, began with the complicated decision to leave a job I loved in Pennsylvania to live closer to my aging parents in Missouri.

I made the move just in time to be there for my eighty-two-year-old mother's two falls, my ninety-year-old father's heartbreaking transition to living in a memory care home, and to share with my brother the necessary but poignant process of helping my mother sell our beloved childhood home. The work of the Oasis Institute is incredibly synchronous with the choices, interventions, supports, and behavior changes that help older adults age successfully. But even with all of those resources and professional associations at my fingertips once I resumed my role there, I still often feel helpless in the face of feelings of loss as I watch my wonderful parents age.

Ken has the ineffable ability to see, and to describe, the internal dialogue of grief and loss. I think this is both because he has metabolized the crushing weight of loss in his own life, and because he is a man incapable of small talk. He wants to share with others what he is feeling and thinking in the most vulnerable way, and he approaches groups as well as individuals with a genuine interest in their internal dialogue and emotional truth.

As I read through *Raising an Aging Parent*, I felt truly "seen" by Ken.

Days after reading the book, I continued to reflect on Ken's words: "How could we not be sad watching the man or woman we saw as a larger-than-life superhero needing our help to get to the bathroom." My eyes welled up as I juxtaposed my previous day's visit to see my father. I helped him stand up for dinner while childhood memories of him danced in front of me. I watched him portage a canoe while carrying two impossibly heavy packs, coach my little league and youth soccer teams, and defeat all of his friends at arm wrestling.

Ken writes about how we can "Heal from Our Deepest Pain," and the importance of making peace with your aging parents. In doing so, he reminded me how lucky I was to have my parents, Barbara and Guido as *my* parents. My decision to move closer to them was predicated more on emotion than logic. They had been spectacularly supportive parents, always engaged in my education, my athletics, the perils of my awkward adolescence, and shared my successes and disappointments. My father, the mathematician, may not have been the best communicator, but my mother's serious and empathic engagement with me and my brother more than filled any voids. They had completely different styles of parenting, but there was never any doubt that I was loved. Ken reminded me that our parents might not always be who we wanted them to be, but that now may be the perfect time to let go of those expectations. It's time to focus on their second half of life and do the best we can to be there for them.

One day, I will no longer be able to call my mother and talk to her about my day, share my wins and losses, tell stories, and listen to hers. Ken's advice and admonitions about unearthing and releasing resentments was humbling—it made me realize how lucky I was and how unique my parents truly are.

Ken Druck is a healer who has mastered the art of guiding us through the losses that are embedded in the fragile human experience—and seizing the opportunities that are there for us and our families as we all get older. May you find abundant love, guidance, forgiveness, gratitude, peace and perspective in the pages ahead.

—PAUL WEISS, President of The Oasis Institute and leader in the creation of the National Family Caregiving Corps

Author's Note

Dear Reader,

I feel that before you begin reading, it's important for you to learn a little about me and how certain events in my life have shaped the direction and path I've taken, which eventually led me to create this book.

Shortly after 9/11, I was asked to lead a series of town hall meetings, support groups, and coaching sessions with the families of those who had died. On one occasion, I found myself standing in front of a thousand people, faced with the task of healing shattered hearts, lives, families, and communities that had been decimated by shameless acts of terrorism. I looked out at the vast, grief-stricken crowd and asked, "Please raise your hand if you feel more heartsick than you'd ever imagined a human being could feel." A thousand people raised their hands.

Then I told those present the story of something that had happened in my own life. In 1996, while participating in a study abroad program in India, my twenty-one-year-old daughter, Jenna, and three other young women tragically died when the bus they were riding to the Taj Mahal overturned. My life as I knew it had ended, and I discovered that I would have to slowly fight my way back into a new life, breath by breath. To honor Jenna, I founded the Jenna Druck Center, a nonprofit organization that provides support and healing to bereaved families and trains young women to be future leaders, using a program my daughter created at age sixteen.

With the love and support of my community, the Jenna Druck Center grew in size and scope over eighteen years, and I found myself helping those, like me and my family, whose loved ones had died in tragedies like 9/11, Columbine, the Boston Marathon, and Sandy Hook. I've had the honor of directly helping many hundreds of families move from their first moments, days, months, and years of darkness back into the light. I have been a regular guest on CNN and PBS specials, sharing everything I have learned about resilience and overcoming life's most challenging adversities.

When I became a father, I dedicated myself to becoming the best possible father I could be, starting with being in the delivery room to assist my wife in the births of our children (which was prohibited back in 1975). Sitting in the waiting room, handing out cigars was not my idea of hands-on fathering. I ended up writing a book called *The Secrets Men Keep* and, as my girls grew older, the challenges I faced as a parent began to evolve. I began writing *How to Talk to Your Kids*, published years later, which was as much an education for me as it was for my readers and the audiences we reached on shows like *The

Author's Note

Oprah Winfrey Show and *The Phil Donahue Show*. And it was no different in the years following Jenna's death, when I spent literally thousands of hours writing about healing after loss in *The Real Rules of Life: Balancing Life's Terms with Our Own*.

In every season of my life, I have sought to bring newfound understanding and courage to the challenges of that time, trying to make sense of what I've gone through and then help others turn pain and adversity into opportunities for becoming their better selves. As I turned sixty-five and began facing some of the new challenges of getting older—including my worn-out knee—my life became, once again, an inquiry. Looking inward and out into the world we live in, I wrote a new book called *Courageous Aging: Your Best Years Ever Reimagined*. During a segment I did with Prince William and Prince Harry about their mother's death, CNN's Don Lemon said, "I've got to read this book." That comment sent me to the Amazon best-seller list. Shortly after, I was invited to do a PBS special and began giving Courageous Aging workshops and leading "Community Conversations on Aging" around the US.

Traveling around our great nation, I have learned a lot about what adult children go through as their parents age. Of course, this topic couldn't have been more resonant for me. Caring for my mother and transitioning out of my seventy-hour-a-week life at the Jenna Druck Center, everything was beginning to shift. In fact, it felt as though I had at least three lives going on—as a son, a nonprofit executive, and a man in his sixties turning the page of his own life.

As I searched for the best way to navigate this new season, writing articles like "What Time Is it (in Your Life)?" for *Costco Connection* magazine, I noticed I was not alone. One of my blog posts, "Watching Your Parents Get Older," also drew enthusiastic responses from readers across the country who were asking important questions about raising their aging parents. And writing this book, I realized, could provide some of the answers.

At first, I thought *Raising an Aging Parent* would be a book only for the adult children of aging parents. But gradually I realized that this is also a book for aging parents themselves. Over the course of my life, I have worked in the trenches and on the frontlines with families. Now is no different. This book is for aging parents and their adult children—and grandchildren too.

Grandchildren witness the relationship between their parents and grandparents, and between their parents and aunts and uncles. And they often step up in remarkable ways to bring their families closer together. Having a relationship with their grandparents that may be difficult or impossible for their parents is not uncommon. Grandparents are often able to express love for grandkids they have never been able to give their own children. (I've learned this personally, after holding my twin grandsons moments after they were born in the final days of writing this book.) *Raising an Aging Parent* is written for every member of the family.

With that said, it's also important to recognize what this book isn't. It's not a race with a finish line in which the adult children assert themselves as caregivers over their parents. Rather,

Author's Note

it's about forging a real-time relationship between adults and their parents, while doing everything possible to improve the quality of life for our families. It's also about making peace between adult children and their parents. Before we dive in further, I do want to make note of one thing—I recognize that there are some relationships with a parent (or even siblings or other family members) that are just irreparable. I have a lot more to say about this in Chapter 4 but I wanted you to know right off the bat that this book is also about *your* journey towards making peace. Many of us have adopted close friends, cousins, neighbors or even co-workers as our "chosen family" and may want to focus on ways we can deepen these relationships.

In the chapters ahead, we will define the playing field of challenges and opportunities that exist between aging parents and adult children—the benefits of communicating clearly, finding forgiveness, remaining flexible and humble, allowing imperfection, and summoning newfound understanding. It will be your job to draw from each chapter, make what you are reading relevant to your situation, and create a plan for your family with best practices to guide you.

May you cultivate boundless love, gratitude, forgiveness, and understanding in your family in the days to come.

Gratefully,
Dr. Ken Druck

Introduction

I joke with my friends' kids, "It's not easy raising a parent," and they smile, knowing full well what I mean. Tongue-in-cheek comments like, "Yeah, my mom's a handful" and "My dad's finally growing up," confirm that our kids really do raise us.

Stringing together lessons from their friends, cousins, grandparents, television sitcoms, and psychology classes, our children learn to become our caregivers, cheerleaders, coaches, rescuers, and—in some cases—our enablers. Through early childhood, the teen years, young adulthood, and a host of difficult transitional periods, these self-appointed caregivers make it up as they go, raising their parents. Some highlights of a parent-raising career may include: high school graduation; leaving for college; getting married; and starting their own families; helping parents adjust to an empty nest; supporting parents through a midlife crisis (or two); retirement; the death of the parents' own parents, siblings, and partners; and their moving out of the family home. As our parents get older, the decline in their physical health and cognitive abilities can be unsettling, and the job of raising a parent can become extremely demanding.

Some of our kids cringe as they watch us get older. They become more distant as we become a little more needy. The reality that we are aging and one day we're going to die is just too much for them to deal with. While some of our children move away or distance themselves emotionally, some do just the opposite; they move in closer and get involved in the work of taking care of their aging mom or dad, or both. Taking care of a parent becomes the organizing principle of these caregivers' lives and a source of deep satisfaction. Too often, however, this leads to a significant diminishing of the care they give, in turn, to their own families, their own health and their careers, and they put themselves at risk of losing the very things that define their own lives.

Regardless of whether our adult children are distant or close, the pressure to get involved in a parent's life increases with the age of the parents. Parents who are beginning to look and feel older, slow down, unplug from a career, face a new season of life—and whose needs are changing—may look to their adult children for support. The parent who once gave care is now in need of care. Merriam-Webster officially added a term for this to its dictionary in 2006: the sandwich generation is "a generation of people (usually in their forties to seventies) who are caring for their aging parents while supporting their own children." You'll see that I refer to them as "SanGen." Adult "SanGen" children, or "sandwich generation" sons and daughters, are called into action no matter how busy their own lives are.

Introduction

The changes that come with age can be deeply unsettling and disheartening. We might prefer to bury our heads in the proverbial sand and not think about them, but we know better. The risks of denial and avoidance can be treacherous, and the emotional and physical debts we incur by "not paying the bills" will eventually come due.

Whether you find yourself raising an aging parent or you are an aging parent who wants a closer relationship with your adult children, this book covers every aspect of how adult children, aging parents, and families can meet these challenges, seize opportunities, make the most of their time together, and pay the good in their lives forward. And since relationships live on long after a parent has died, you'll also find advice herein for those who may wish to make peace with a deceased parent. While I may refer to something that's happening with one of your parents in the pages ahead, some of you are dealing with matters that involve both of your parents; if that's the case, please read on with both parents in mind.

If you find something in any of the coming chapters that you would like to take a step further, please visit my web site www.kendruck.com where you will find a treasure trove of articles, coaching tips and programs for moving forward. To make it easier to record your insights while you're reading this book and keep a personal history of your thoughts and action steps, we've also created a companion workbook, *Raising and Aging Parent Journal*.

Chapter 1
There's Nothing Easy About Watching Your Parents Get Older

Making peace with our parents was the focus of my generation in the '60s, '70s and '80s. Trained in the fine art of giving my clients "parentectomies" to help them differentiate who they were, separate and apart from their mothers and fathers, I sensed that life for many of them seemed like an endless summer. Then, as I got older, had kids of my own, and joined my clients in watching our parents get older, the game changed.

Our roles slowly began to reverse and we found ourselves raising our parents. Many of us started to become our aging mother's and father's caregivers, watching over them, supporting them through difficult transitions, and helping them make hard decisions.

The opportunities for having a special closeness with an aging mother or father adds immeasurably to the quality of our lives and theirs. On the other hand, the challenges of raising an aging parent can be maddening, time-consuming, and heart-wrenching. How we go about facing these challenges and harvesting these opportunities depends on our willingness and ability to operate from an effective playbook.

You may have seen your mom or dad retire, suffer a health crisis, slow down physically, or face a financial challenge in recent years. And it hit you for the first time that they are becoming the older version of themselves. You and your siblings may already be knee-deep in the issues of aging, where your aging parents are looking to you for help as they try to downsize their home, fine-tune their estate plans, and adjust to health challenges. Or your parents may already be in a state of decline, requiring considerable support and doing their best as they edge toward the end of life. Or perhaps you are looking back at your relationships with your parents now that they are gone, trying to understand and reconcile a time that has passed.

How could we not be sad watching the man or woman we saw as a larger-than-life superhero needing our help to get to the bathroom or connect with their grandchildren? How painful it is, taking away the car keys from the person who drove us everywhere but has now become a menace behind the wheel. The wise and attentive mother or father who seemed to know everything now seems to be unable to remember anything,

There's Nothing Easy About Watching Your Parents Get Older

including which pill to take at what hour. And these changes aren't happening in a vacuum. You have your own life: the demands of a family, job, finances, or even health issues. It's not like you or your siblings have all the time in the world to step away from your own lives to take care of mom and dad. But you're probably doing it anyway.

Taking care of your parents is the right thing to do. Much as they might not want to admit it, they need your help. Without you, they might have great difficulty sorting out legal, medical, financial and psychological matters. But caregiving comes at a cost. It's all too easy to forget your own needs when you're focused on somebody else's. And you want to do everything in your power to protect your own family, health and sanity in the process.

Some of us, including those who went to therapy, are also still dealing with parent issues. We didn't get along particularly well with our parents and there's still a lot of unfinished business, unexpressed anger, unresolved conflicts, hurt and guilt standing in our way. And issues that linger on into our adulthood can have a profound effect on how we relate to our aging parents.

We may be so angry and distrusting that we're unwilling to care for them or so fearful and compliant that we fail to factor our own self-care into the equation. And to complicate matters still further, we may have a brother or sister with their own ideas about how to treat mom and/or dad, where they should live, and what to do with their money. Every family is different, as is every parent–child relationship. Each situation demands its own line of critical thinking and decision-making. And when there's only one sibling, the planning process is even more essential.

Whether you have an open line of communication with your parents and can talk to them about almost anything, or you are working to achieve that sort of openness, your parents in all likelihood will need you and your siblings. No matter what happened earlier, they are, and will always be, your mom and dad. Things will evolve with each transition, from their retirement to their first encounter with a serious health issue, to other kinds of unwelcome changes. As the changes come, you will have an opportunity to decide and do what's right. This might mean taking the so-called high road of forgiving them and showing up in their time of need. It might be a matter of setting clear terms and conditions for your involvement. It could also mean realizing that you cannot be their caregiver and stepping back from the situation.

> There's nothing easy about raising an aging parent—or being one. The rewards, benefits and blessings of being a good son or daughter, and giving your parents your best shot, cannot be underestimated.

There's nothing easy about raising an aging parent—or being one. The rewards, benefits and blessings of being a good son or daughter, and giving your parents your best shot, cannot be underestimated. Whether you are reading this book for yourself, your parents, your siblings, or maybe

There's Nothing Easy About Watching Your Parents Get Older

even your kids, you're on a journey through the grand cycle of life. There's a good chance that one day you'll be an aging parent, aunt, uncle, or mentor yourself. The loving kindness, patience, support, love, and encouragement that come your way may make all the difference as you face life's challenging "fourth quarter."

You've made the decision to pick up this book because you want to do the right thing. In these pages you will find an answer to that incredibly complicated question: "What now; what kind of a son or daughter am I going to be?" To begin to answer that question, let me tell you what happened in my relationship with my own mother and what I learned from the experience.

My mother was quite a character. She lived a good and full life. My love for and understanding of Roslyn Druck continues to grow three years after her life ended. All the way back in 1939, before she was married, my mother—as Rozzie Schuster—performed at the World's Fair in New York, playing her clarinet. She also loved the piano and performed classical pieces by the great masters. My Mom went to college and ended up going into an exciting new medium called radio. I have stunning photographs of her from that era, when she was a beautiful young brunette. They also capture a preview of what came next for her, graduating at the top of her class, marrying Lieutenant Charles Druck, and having three adoring children. The pictures show her happy, becoming a mom, and with her parents and family during the holidays.

Slowly, over time, the pictures also show my mother getting older, passing through all the phases of her life. When my dad died at age sixty-nine—my age as I write this book—she moved into a beautiful complex called North Shore Towers, where she thrived on being a loving "Bubby," or grandma, leading community coat drives for the homeless, going to concerts and lectures with her friends, and playing the piano and an occasional game of golf. She made her first and only hole in one at age seventy-four! As she grew still older and could no longer fend for herself, my sister, Roberta, who lived nearby, became her caregiver.

The cold New York weather was taking a toll on her, so she eventually decided to move to California to live near me, her grandchildren, and our growing West Coast family. Together, we found a wonderful retirement community, and my sister traveled with her for the move to help complete the transition. I'll never forget the moment when I dropped off my sister at the airport for her return to New York. She tapped me on the shoulder, the way she had when we were six or seven years old. "You're it," she declared, and she meant it. I became my mom's caregiver until the day she died, nine years later.

*　*　*

My mother lived to be ninety-two, and I feel lucky to have been such a special part of her day-to-day life. I watched her pass through so many seasons of life, even though the very last one was painfully difficult for her and for all of us. A

There's Nothing Easy About Watching Your Parents Get Older

few years after she had relocated to California, I began to get urgent calls from her in the middle of the night. At first those calls were rare, but they grew more frequent. At two or three in the morning I would find her on the floor, and I would lift her gently and carry her to the bathroom. Every time I left, my heart hurt. I didn't want to see my mother suffer that way.

My mother's mind and body were wearing out and beginning to fail. It was deeply unsettling, unpleasant, and even demeaning to find my mother on the floor needing assistance getting to the toilet. But I would grow to realize that this is what happens in the cycle of life. Facing it is what it means to be a good son.

If you reflect on this, you will notice that this transition to becoming parental caregivers and begins long before your parents ever need your help. In a sense, this seasonal change, as I call it, was already underway when you took your first steps toward independence—maybe when your parents dropped you off at kindergarten at age five. Or it began when you left home for the first time at age eighteen, hugged your mom goodbye, and saw tears in her eyes. These were special moments, but bittersweet because your parents had to let go. Even way back then, things were beginning to shift. As you left home, your family entered a new season, and for the first time you began to develop adult relationships with your mother and father. They had always been the protectors, pillars of strength and security, rule makers and caregivers, but now that was changing. You were reassuring them things were going to be okay.

In some families, these changes begin long before a child moves out, especially if the parents suffer from addiction or other forms of physical or mental illness. Children of alcoholic parents, for instance, know from a very young age that their parents need help, and they try to intervene. The kids begin parenting the parents, sometimes when they're just a few years old.

Almost no one realizes it at the time, but within that first transition to independence is the seed of a much later stage of life. When Dad stands with us at our wedding, we're already halfway to the day when we become the adult and he is the one in need of care. We leave home and milestones start piling up quickly.

We start to hear whispers about our parents' health troubles. In my case, that part of the story happened very early. My dad had a heart attack at age thirty-five, when I was still a little kid. A telling glance from my mother was sufficient to let me know my father was not well and not to stress him. For most kids, however, the signs that our parents are human come later. But whenever they come, they're signals that our parents are not as strong as they once were. They are vulnerable, and they need us. Meanwhile, our own lives are busy; we're building our careers and having children of our own, who as they get older, will begin living out their own lives.

A few years ago, after a long and storied career playing club soccer, putting many hard miles on my body, my right knee finally gave out. The cartilage had worn away and it was bone on bone, so I had horrible arthritis and was walking with a terrible limp. I started noticing the way my daughter was looking at me.

There's Nothing Easy About Watching Your Parents Get Older

I watched her watching me. I could actually see her realizing, maybe for the first time in her life, that her daddy had gotten older and that I was not going to be around forever.

My dad had died many years before, and I had watched my mom grow older. Now I was next on what my Uncle Larry called "the conveyor belt." After catching my daughter seeing her old man as an old man, I noticed subtle changes in how she spoke to me. She had always been a wise counselor to her daddy, but she was taking more time to parent me. She started gently reminding me to take care of myself, and even started calling me "Papa." I was no longer her spry forty-year-old daddy. I had been through many hard seasons of a very full life and I was changing. Atop the list of changes, I was going to be a grandfather. I liked my new title.

That's the cycle of life. It's normal and it's healthy—but it isn't easy. When the time comes for each of us to begin raising our aging parents, both challenges and opportunities spring up from every direction.

A Disarming Realization— and the Challenges That Follow

We can never fully prepare for the moment when we realize that we are becoming our parents' caretakers. Though the signs may have been there for years, the moment of realization can still come as a shock. Whether they acknowledge it or not, the people we depended upon for our very survival now depend on us. We are now watching over and protecting them.

Perhaps it's nothing more than a watchful eye, making sure they're eating properly. Or it may be more serious, with us making sure there's a roof over their heads and supporting them financially. They may be turning to us as a confidant, depending on us as a lifeline to stave off feelings of loneliness and despair. It may feel like it's now on us to provide them with a sense of safety and security. We're doing many of the things we would do for a child. It may be disconcerting and uncomfortable, or a welcome change we feel they have earned.

As we may discover while raising some of our children, aging parents who are resistant to accepting help or whose needs are considerable can be especially challenging. I call them "Special Needs Aging Parents," or "SNAPs." Adult children who become caregivers for their parents may consider it to be a burden, a blessing or a little of both. "Raising" a child means to help them grow up, but the word *raise* also means to elevate, and the opportunity to raise an aging parent can be a chance to elevate someone who has made many, many sacrifices for us. In some parts of the world, like India, it's often considered an honor to be the caregiver of an aging parent. Adult children compete to be the trusted child with whom the aging parent resides. Caring for parents in such a country conveys a kind of status.

In contrast, cultures like ours view "old people" as having little or no value, and our discomfort with aging and death can make it hard to watch, or get involved, during our parents' final years. After my mother relocated to California and I started

There's Nothing Easy About Watching Your Parents Get Older

getting those calls in the middle of the night, it was terrible. Messy. Uncomfortable. Inconvenient. Exhausting. Sad and frightening. My mother's body was failing her.

I tried to brighten her every day with phone calls, visits, and field trips to the beach for a sunset, the symphony for some Dvořák, and our home for special family gatherings. Not only did I feel guilty about not doing more to help my mother, it was also unsettling to see other once-brilliant, talented, and successful eighty-five and ninety-year-old men and women trying valiantly to get around in walkers, sitting alone looking into space, and dining together with little or nothing to say. I could not bear to imagine myself in such bad shape at that age—yet, of course, I knew it was a possibility.

At times, I must admit, it was easier to get lost in the day-to-day busyness of my own life than to go visit my mother and the other elderly residents. At the height of my discomfort, I would think about all that my mother had done for me when I was a child. She now needed her son's loving touch and smile. I hated seeing her in such a fragile state—but how many times had she changed my diaper? I was now doing for her what she had done for me.

Had she always wanted to change a screaming child's diaper? This was a woman who had played the clarinet in front of crowds at the World's Fair, who had taken on the role of proud matriarch of our family when my dad died, who sat with me in front of my junior high school guidance counselor as he told her, "Don't worry, Mrs. Druck, your boy can always become a janitor or something," and who had flown overnight across the country to watch me receive my doctorate.

Surely, there were plenty of times when she would have preferred to be out living her own life rather than wiping my rear end, but she had made those sacrifices for me. And now, I decided, it was my turn. That perspective of being a good son and it being my turn to take care of and selflessly serve my mother would help me as time wore on, because there were plenty of trials ahead of us.

Raising an aging parent is also challenging because of our parents' discomfort with their new season of life. They are proud and accustomed to being independent and self-sufficient. At some point, perhaps not very long ago, they may have begun to go through a change. It could be as subtle as having to face the older version of themselves in the mirror—gray hair, wrinkles, and all—or as life-altering as having to go through a health crisis, retire, face an empty nest, or lose a close friend. These kinds of transitions generally bring with them a host of new challenges.

Aging parents may also begin to go through significant mental and physical changes and start accepting our assistance. A close friend who used to brag about how fiercely independent her mom had become since her dad's passing, told me, "My mom's heart problems have changed everything. She has nonstop appointments and needs me to drive her. It's thrown everything off-kilter. There goes my life. I know that my mom's loss of independence has been painful and frightening.

Thankfully, she is dealing with these changes, owning up to how difficult this transition is, and accepting my help."

While aging parents' resistance to getting help may be the most difficult part of this stage, it, too, is entirely understandable. They're afraid—and who wouldn't be? Everything, including their identity, status, and source of self-worth is waning, and they aren't sure what comes next. They may also resist because they fear becoming a burden. Taught to be staunchly self-reliant, they watch their adult children living busy lives, and so they may hide, deny, repress, or camouflage their own needs.

Accepting help may also threaten their status. They are the matriarch or patriarch of the family and they want to maintain that position. They don't want to be seen as a lesser version of themselves and demoted. We need to understand and appreciate how hard it is for them to let go of the way things look, and how important it is for them to maintain their independence.

"Help? What makes you think I need help?" one workshop attendee's father barked at him when he asked his dad if he could be of any help after hip-replacement surgery. I have watched an aging father on oxygen, his body wracked from battling lung cancer, and yet he professed not to need any help. Aging parents can build a fortress of denial around what's happening to them. Despite that fortress, inwardly they may feel sad, scared, lost, alone, ashamed, embarrassed, or simply inhibited to ask for what they really need.

We must define precisely what a healthy caregiver relationship looks like: someone with good communication skills who treats others with mutual respect and sets healthy boundaries and limits. Even while I found a great deal of meaning in caring for my mother, there were times when tough love was the only way to move forward. There were moments when her resistance created chaos in both of our lives, and finally I had to take charge and dictate how we were going to handle a given situation.

Do you remember a time when your children were failing to make good decisions on their own behalf? Like many parents, you probably did something along the lines of giving them "three good options" to choose from. When my mother reached a time in her life when she was not making good decisions, I did the same thing. "Mom, I love you and need you to trust me here. I am giving you three choices," I would declare. As upset as she would become with me, and as scared and defiant as she might have felt, my mother would eventually comply.

Why? Because she knew I loved her and was watching out for her. She knew she could trust me. "Let's figure this out, Mom. We can do better than this," I would say to her. Occasionally, I would coordinate with Mom's doctor and the professional caregivers at the retirement home where she lived to come up with plans that made things safer, simpler, and easier for her, and for everybody else as well.

These kinds of difficult challenges can also create conflict between siblings. Nearly all of us carry some baggage from our

There's Nothing Easy About Watching Your Parents Get Older

family. More often than not, sibling rivalries, jealousies, and differences can start to resurface as parents get older and turn to their children for help. We discover that some or all of our old baggage had simply gone underground, and now—amid this new stress—it comes roaring back to the surface.

This can be yet another source of pain and difficulty on top of what's happening to our aging parents. Siblings can compete for "best son" or "best daughter" status, with grandchildren sometimes used as pawns to win the favor of an aging parent. Sibling wars are always a lose–lose proposition. We'll tackle this in depth in Chapter 6, and throughout this book we'll explore ways in which family members can get ahead of the pain curve by communicating and taking the high road with one another.

Family closeness is one of the many blessings that can come out of this phase of life. As with raising a child, giving our time, attention, and love to an aging parent can be among the most noble and selfless things we ever do. My daily phone calls to my mother, heart-to-heart conversations, spontaneous lunches, beach walks, sunsets, symphonies, and unplanned visits to see her completed a joyful and meaningful spiritual cycle in my own life.

I was able to give life back to my mother. While I miss her terribly, and

> As with raising a child, giving our time, attention, and love to an aging parent can be among the most noble and selfless things we ever do.

things were not perfect, this has left me with a feeling of deep peace. My mother's body eventually gave out, as all bodies do, but my love for her will never die.

Strengthening Family Bonds Is a Gradual Process

It is nearly three years since my mother passed. As I said earlier, I would call her every morning and ask, "How's my favorite mother?" Though she's been gone, I still often ask her that question while driving or on a hike. I miss my mom terribly and feel blessed to have been her son and watched that incredible woman who gave birth to me pass through the seasons of her life—and to have given life back to her. It will go down as one of the great accomplishments of my life to have been a good and loving son.

Raising an aging parent can be a wondrous and rewarding part of the natural cycle of life. It's the cycle in which we will pass our own legacy of love to our children and grandchildren, because raising a parent is also about strengthening the bonds of family between generations—strengthening our nation and our world. This is a journey of building stronger, kinder, more compassionate, and deeply loving families—for our parents, for ourselves, for our children, and for the grandchildren yet to come. It is within our power to achieve that. So let's get started by tackling some of the core challenges that arise as your parents get older.

There's Nothing Easy About Watching Your Parents Get Older

Ready to Get to Work Right Now?

If this chapter has sparked your curiosity or desire to make things better in your family, you can find a series of suggested exercises in the chapters ahead, at the end of this book and in our *Raising an Aging Parent Journal* at www.KenDruck.com.

Chapter 2

Family Role Reversal: Are You Becoming the Parent?

The best, most caring and most affectionate relationships between adult children and their aging parents are the ones that change with the changing seasons of life. Adult children, once the exclusive recipients of their mother's and/or father's protection and care, take on the role of being their parents' caregiver, confidant, helpmate, advocate and advisor.

Aging mothers and fathers, once the all-knowing parents in charge of their children's lives, allow themselves to be taken care of and watched over by their adult children as circumstances change. The adjustments we make in our minds, hearts, and families to a *new normal* as we get older may not be easy. But they are critical when it comes to achieving the highest and best quality of life for our aging parents and ourselves.

I have become good friends with Mel, a spirited ninety-six-year-old who lives in the home next to my office. Mel's wife died a few years back, and as I've gotten to know him, I've been impressed by the active and independent life he leads: He meets with a small group of his buddies a few times a week for lunch or to play golf. Mel is sharp as a tack; he keeps up with the news, reads the latest best-sellers, and always asks about my life when I see him.

Two months ago, Mel fell, broke his hip, and had to undergo surgery. Living in a senior rehabilitation center while his hip was healing, he told me, "A few weeks ago I was playing golf. Now, I'm stuck in this place with a bunch of old folks. I can't even get up and go for a walk until this damn thing heals. I want my old life back."

Burning through a few adventure novels a week, sitting around watching "stupid" television programs, and managing a level of non-activity that was totally uncharacteristic for him dampened Mel's spirits. His sons, both in their sixties, were very concerned. Up until their father's fall, they would check in on him by phone a few times a week and drive to his home for an occasional visit. Now, they visited him in the rehab center almost every weekend, adjusting their lives in every way—to meet their father's needs.

They were accustomed to the dad who had journeyed flawlessly through his sixties, seventies, eighties, and even most of his nineties. Seeing him old and frail was a shock. They were slowly coming face to face with the reality of how much time, energy, and emotional commitment would be required to get their father back on his feet. They put their own lives on

Family Role Reversal: Are You Becoming the Parent?

hold while he recovered, placing their children and spouses on the back burner, and stepped into their new roles as full-time caregivers. It was exhausting, but they did it.

For Mel's family, the change happened suddenly. For many of us, however, the adult child/aging parent role reversal happens very gradually. Those who live close to their parents and see them regularly may not even notice the way this change creeps into the relationship. We may not even be aware of the degree to which we have begun to take responsibility for our parents. It may start with driving them where they need to go or overseeing their finances. Before we know it, we start making arrangements for whatever they need—appointments, home maintenance, medications, the whole gamut. It happens slowly over a long period, until one day we discover that a basic reversal of roles has taken place. And it's probably never going to go back to the way it was.

As I pointed out earlier, some of us feel like we've been playing the parental role for as long as we can remember. Maybe we grew up in a dysfunctional household and took the reins of responsibility as early as we possibly could. Or perhaps we were the oldest sibling and always had to babysit the younger ones. As our parents start to require more care, we may feel like we've worn this suit before; as far as we're concerned, we've spent our entire lives taking care of, compensating for, watching over, and parenting our parents.

For people who live far from their parents, the role reversal can strike like a lightning bolt. And, regardless of whether you assume this role suddenly or gradually—or whether you've been doing it in some sense for your entire life—taking care of our aging parents marks a deeply significant change in our family. We are now the caregiver. We are starting conversations with our mother about her well-being even though she was the one who took care of us, or was supposed to. Those roles have reversed, and it can be both jarring and awkward.

Some of us were spoiled by our parents. Warmed by our mother's wise, loving, caring words, and surrounded by her protective arms we grew extremely dependent on her—and we don't want to give that up. Others have been waiting, wishing that somehow, someway, they would one day hear the words, "I love you, and I'm so proud of you," or receive the loving care they yearned for from mom or dad. Regardless of the challenges you may find yourself facing as you try to come to terms with your new caregiving role and responsibilities, here are three steps taken from other people's family playbooks that can help you make the transition.

Step One: Fully Acknowledge What Is Happening

Whether it's something you've been quietly managing for many years or a sudden change brought on by a crisis, now is the time to step back and acknowledge that a role reversal is taking place between you and your parents. If going through this change is turning your world inside out, take a moment to admit it. Admitting it to yourself and then to a trusted friend or confidant that your parent is experiencing a decline

Family Role Reversal: Are You Becoming the Parent?

in their health, memory, ability to function independently, etc. may be painfully difficult and terribly sad. It is natural and understandable for you to feel completely unmoored, uncertain as to how to proceed, even furious that life can be so unfair and make things so hard. All of these feelings are natural and normal.

Even if you feel as though you've been taking care of your parent for a very long time, this is still an important opportunity to stop and take inventory, appreciating yourself and your siblings for what you have done over all these years. Step back and acknowledge the sacrifices you have made and how much you have contributed to the quality of your parent's life. It's also a perfect time to consider what it has cost you. In addition to understanding how difficult things have been for your parents as they have gotten older, take the time to reflect on what has transpired between you and your aging parents, the challenges you have faced together, and the toll it has taken on you and your siblings.

Step Two: Evaluate: How Is This Working Out for Me?
While you may have assumed a caregiving role in order to respond to your parent's needs—health care, financial, emotional, logistical, etc.—you may not have given much consideration to how it has, or will, affect you and your siblings. So, let me ask, "How is it affecting you that they are getting older? Are you being visited by a sense of guilt, obligation, responsibility, or perhaps a desire to be more a part of their

lives? If so, how? How is all of this, including the things you're already doing to help them, affecting *you*? And how is it affecting your family? Is one of your parents, a sibling, or your partner telling you that you should become more involved in helping your parents? Are you questioning anybody, telling them they should become more involved? How so?"

If you're the adult child, you may be feeling happy and proud of the way you've shown up for your parents at such a challenging time. If you're the aging parent, you may also be feeling happy and proud of how things are going with your adult children. Perhaps one of your children is a natural-born caregiver, showing you how much they love you and how devoted they are to your well-being, while another one of your kids seems to have gone missing, has become resentful, or is suffocating you.

Understanding how the changes in our life and our parents' lives are affecting us leads us to clear thinking about how to best address the new normal. Rather than accepting that this is "just the way it is," running around with our hair on fire, and/or being seduced into a quick-fix solution, we will now explore the best possible scenario for our relationship with our aging parent.

Step Three: Ask the Right Questions—of Ourselves

Raising an aging parent and showing them the love and respect we would want requires reflection. Ask yourself this question: If it all ended right now, what would I regret about the way I handled things? How might I wish I'd acted differently?

Family Role Reversal: Are You Becoming the Parent?

Maybe you'd wish you'd taken better care of them during this difficult time. Or perhaps you'd wish that you had forgiven your parent for something you allowed to affect you, or that you had taken a different approach in involving your siblings. If it ended today, would you wish that you had been a more loving, forgiving, accepting, or supportive son or daughter? *Is what I'm doing right now the best, smartest and most loving version of me as a son or daughter?*

> Raising an aging parent and showing them the love and respect we would want requires reflection. Ask yourself this question: If it all ended right now, what would I regret about the way I handled things? How might I wish I'd acted differently?

Then there's the issue of self-care. How might I wish I had taken better care of myself? Could I have shown myself greater respect, appreciation, kindness, understanding and permission to break free of guilt? Did I allow myself to be blinded or influenced by fear, shame, denial, or judgment? How might I have broken free of these things—even if it meant surrendering a long-held hope for my mother or father's love and affection?

These questions are not easy. They can be especially painful because most of us run into pockets of old anger and resentment when we start to examine our relationships with our parents. Pain from early childhood has a way of lingering into adulthood. Your parents may have been nearly perfect as you grew up, in which case your cup is overflowing with gratitude and appreciation. Or they may not have been available or accountable in the ways that you needed and wanted when you were young. Your attempts to reach them on an emotional level may have been successful throughout your childhood and into your adult years, or they may have been repeatedly rebuffed. Your parents may have been abusive, distant or manipulative, and they may have sent you mixed messages—inviting you to come closer, and then shunning you when you did.

Some people are just not hardwired to be loving, nurturing, supportive parents. Parents who are stark raving narcissists do not know how to set limits, mentor, coach, love and guide their children. Your mom and dad may have been a model for who you ultimately wanted to become in the world, or your parent may have been the opposite of what you wanted to emulate. For reasons we will leave to in-depth psychoanalysis, your mother or father probably did their level best. And as a result of that, you have been left with a variety of feelings from gratitude and affection, to anger and sorrow.

Now, as you grapple with this new phase of caregiving, you may feel these things rising up. You may feel resentful, indifferent, and detached. Watching what's happening to your mom or dad, some part of you wants to throw up your hands and say, "I don't owe you anything. After what you've put me through, you expect me to step up and do this? No, thanks." And you could justify doing nothing at all.

On the other hand, you may find yourself tearfully remembering heartwarming scenes from your childhood, sharing moments of belly laughter from family trips, or planning an adventure your dad took you on with your own son or daughter. If so, your heart swells with joy and deep gratitude.

It is understandable that these kinds of mixed emotions arise as our parents get older. How could you not feel this way? How could you not feel grateful or angry? How could you not feel like saying, "Thank you!" or "To hell with them!"? The question we need to consider in the midst of either painful emotions or swells of gratitude is, "What will it take for me to make peace with how things worked out with my parents?"

Now that you have come to terms with what's happening in your life and your aging parents' lives, moving forward involves exploring challenging emotions, summoning courage to deal with lingering issues, and offering yourself as much compassion as you would a friend going through similar life circumstances.

Healing from Our Deepest Pain

Processing the emotions that arise as our parents get older, or those that arise in us as aging parents when we reflect back on the peaks and valleys of our lives, helps clear the path forward. Are you experiencing these kinds of feelings as your parents get older? What are they? What brought them on? Might it help you to talk about something that happened (or something that never happened) in order to fortify the process of making peace with your parents or your adult children?

The answers to these questions may be hidden in your persisting anger, indifference, fear or tears. Purging yourself of the disappointment or despair that you've carried for so many years and acknowledging the unmet needs of the little girl or little boy who really could have used a more attentive, less self-involved or insecure parent is often achieved with the help of skilled therapists. Special programs like the Hoffman Process help countless thousands of people release childhood trauma and create positive changes in their lives. Dealing with the issues that linger and stand in the way of making peace with your aging parents can present an important opportunity.

Acknowledging these feelings is something you are doing for your own edification and will not necessarily involve talking to your parent. Searching for an inner reconciliation, with a hand on your own heart, you now acknowledge the parts of yourself that wished for something other than what you got. Perhaps you yearned for a mom who could have talked to you when you needed it. Or a dad who could have set a better example of the man you wanted to become. Much as we might all want a redo, or another chance to meet the unmet needs of our childhood, that's now history. To what degree we hold ourselves in esteem and what happens from here on out is now happening on our watch.

Becoming your parent's caregiver may necessitate the need and internal decision to let go of the wishes we have carried around since childhood—that our mom or dad would finally be the parent we always wanted them to be. Now may be the perfect

Family Role Reversal: Are You Becoming the Parent?

time to let go of old expectations. In many ways this process is akin to psychoanalysis, which allows people to reconcile and release the anger and disappointment they've felt toward their parents, recalibrate their expectations, and take better care of themselves by setting healthy limits when they are with their now aging parents. "No more buying into mixed messages," they say to themselves. "No more inviting me in for hugs and then sticking your elbows in my chest. It is what it is!" Or maybe, they are thinking, "Mom, I resent you for not finding another partner and for depending so heavily on me." There's a long laundry list of anger and disappointment anyone may have.

It was what it was, and our parents are who they are. Making peace can be tough—so is acknowledging that you would have chosen a parent who was more attuned to your feelings and could have said and done more of the kinds of things you needed. You got the parents that you got. So did they. Again, with a hand over your own heart, acknowledge the needs of the child who might not have gotten the love and attention he or she really needed. Acknowledge, too, your aging parent who went through their own trials and tribulations as a child and probably did the very best they could as an adult.

Finding constructive outlets for expressing what you feel, acknowledging what you needed, and telling your story opens more space in your heart. Hearts will break; this is unavoidable. Whether they break open or closed is another matter. I am not suggesting that letting our hearts break open and heal is something that happens instantly or swiftly. But, eventually, with the pain and despair purged, you may discover some breathing room. And a few heart-warming thank-yous:

"Thank you, Mom, for giving me life."

"Thank you, Dad, for the time you smiled and told me I was a good boy."

"Thank you, Mom and Dad, for all the ways you loved your grandkids."

Summoning Newfound Courage

If you are a parent, take a moment to think back on the birth of your first child. That was probably a sacred and unforgettable day; you may remember it as the most incredible day of your life, as I do. As you think back on that time, can you remember if your child's arrival in this world gave you a kind of high that is unequaled in this life? You held this beautiful newborn and discovered that you loved this tiny person more than you thought possible—and at the same time, you felt overwhelmed, even terrified, by the weight of your responsibility.

You may have asked yourself, consciously or not, "What kind of parent am I going to be? Am I up to this task? What if I don't know what to do?" In that moment, many of us are forced to look at ourselves in a way we never have before. In becoming a parent, we know that we have to show up, grow up, find newfound strength, and tap into the very best of ourselves.

Raising an aging parent can bring a similar feeling. First, we acknowledge the journey we've been on since childhood,

Family Role Reversal: Are You Becoming the Parent?

growing up and interacting with the parents who gave us life. And now, facing the reality of our parents' advancing age, we have a reckoning with who we are as a daughter or son. Just as bringing a child into this world is an awesome responsibility, so, too, is holding our mother or father close as they age and eventually pass from this life. Just as you grappled with who you were when you first held your newborn child, this is a moment to ask, "What kind son or daughter am I? How can I rise to the challenges of raising my aging parent? When this is over, will I know that I did my very best?"

We slowly let go of the question, "Who is my parent and how did they show up for me in my time of greatest need?" Now we ask instead, "Who am I, and how am I going to show up for my mother or father in their time of greatest need?"

Again, I don't pretend that these are easy questions to face, or that raising an aging parent is a walk in the park. As fears and uncertainties arise in us, we ask ourselves the following questions:

"Is this now my responsibility? If so, can I handle it?"

"What parts of this am I not prepared to face?"

"In what ways do I feel unprepared or even inadequate for this task?"

"How might this be triggering my own fears of aging?"

* * *

My own father had always been a pillar of strength, but due to rheumatic fever as a child, there came a time when his heart began to fail. There were a few times in his sixties when we rushed him to the hospital. He had lost a tremendous amount of weight and had become very frail. Facing his own death for the first time, my father looked truly scared.

Standing outside his hospital room, I didn't know if or how I could face my father in that state. I searched for the strength to walk into his room with a smile and say something to help him. Would I be able to summon the courage—a sort of strength that I had never needed until this moment—to sit by his bedside and hold his hand? Would I be able to endure the sight of fear in the eyes of this man who had always been fearless? Could I summon the courage to step up and be the person he needed me to be that day?

The answer to this question will not be the same for everyone. In the end, in my own case, I was able to sit beside my father, hold his hand, listen to and reassure him. For a constellation of reasons, I was in a position to do this. We all struggle with our fears at times like this, and there may be a strong temptation to judge ourselves harshly. But when faced with this moment of truth, each of us does the best we can.

Finding Self-Compassion

All too often, we beat ourselves up for things we didn't do or could have done differently. We put ourselves on trial in an imaginary courtroom with no jury and no defense. There is only a prosecutor waving an admonishing finger of blame in our face and piling on evidence of our failings.

Family Role Reversal: Are You Becoming the Parent?

We find ourselves guilty of falling short as a good son or daughter. Standing convicted and ready for punishment, we cower. But holding ourselves hostage to what we could have done differently, bullying, admonishing, shaming or harshly criticizing ourselves has absolutely no redeeming value. It accomplishes nothing.

It may be time to take your foot off your own throat and move from harsh self-criticism to kindness and self-compassion. This is the path of growth, forgiveness, peace, kindness, humility, and redemption. It is how we grow, heal and ripen as the imperfect sons or daughters we are. From today forward I encourage you to learn the practice self-compassion. While we hold the awareness that we could have done things differently, we must find it in our hearts to accept that we did the best we could and that we are currently doing the best we can. Learning to talk to ourselves with newfound kindness, patience and understanding is one of the most powerful and healing things we can do to start dealing with our families more effectively.

Stepping Into Our New Role/New Normal

In the past few pages, we have described coming to terms with lingering fears and anger, and striving to move from angry gasps and annoyed eye rolls to gracious thank-yous. The next step is to look inward, acknowledging our limitations and offering ourselves forgiveness. With this process underway, we can ask ourselves one of the central questions of this book: "What is the level of care and presence that I can provide in the days ahead so that, if my parent passes tomorrow, I can look back on their final days and be more at peace with myself?"

We're in a moment of choice. In this moment, the task for each of us is to determine our own gold standard of care, to say to ourselves, "This is who I aspire to be as a son or daughter, mother or father." We pledge to move through our anger and resentment and anything else that would hinder us from loving our parent and giving them our kind attention. We step up.

You may be someone who has already gone through this phase of making peace, whether your parent has passed on or is still alive. But whether the challenges of raising your aging parent are in the past, present, or future, there is a way for you to step up right now—today—and take the high road. If your parent has passed, do your best to accept the limitations they had and express gratitude for whatever they were able to give. Over time, you may find that you're able to accept the relationship both for what it was and what it wasn't.

If raising an aging parent is something you're struggling with, then this may be your moment of opportunity. To find out how, ask yourself the following questions:

"What would have to happen for me to let go?"

"To what specific standard of care would I be willing to hold myself?"

"Am I willing to spend quality time with my parents?"

"How do I feel about supporting my parents financially, emotionally, psychologically, and logistically?"

Family Role Reversal: Are You Becoming the Parent?

As part of setting this standard, you may also need to set some healthy boundaries. I remember when my mother moved to California how guilty I could feel at the end of every visit by telling her, "Mom, I have to leave."

When she would respond, "Why can't you stay for lunch? You must have so many more important things to do," it would cast a shadow over our entire visit, and each time I would drive home feeling terrible. Finally, after several visits, I said, "Mom, I love coming to visit you. But you get so upset when I have to go, and I leave feeling bad. So here's what I have decided: From now on, I will call and tell you how much time I have. I will say, 'Mom, I have an hour and a half,' and you can tell me whether that is enough time. If it isn't, I will arrange to visit you on another day when I have two or three hours."

I told my mother it was just too painful to feel that guilt and see her so upset, and I couldn't do that anymore. Finally, I set specific rules. When it was time for me to leave, she could not ask me to stay or invoke any kind of guilt. That was a tough-love limit.

After that, I started calling my mom and asking if today was a good day to visit, and if so, would this amount of time work for her. If she said, "yes," then I would come and we'd have our visit. And at the end, she would watch herself. She learned to bite her tongue. She also liked to remind me how well she was doing.

"You know, I'm following your agreement," she would say.

"I know you are. Thank you, Mom."

In time, my guilt subsided. All that was left were smiles.

In addition to setting limits with your parent, reaching for your gold standard of care may also require you to do some cleanup of your sibling relationships. All too often, there is some kind of drama between brothers and sisters. Perhaps an older sibling acts as the savior and badmouths the other one, who isn't around as much.

Statements like, "Mom, it's a good thing at least one of your adult children takes the time out to call and visit you" can fuel a dangerous sibling rivalry.

This sort of drama triangle is just one type of toxic arrangement in some families. Sibling problems can come in every shape and size. I knew one family in which the daughter lived out of state, and every time she came to visit, she and her aging mother would set each other off and end up in a screaming match. They would find themselves repeating arguments that were fifty years old; the mother would resume her old role, the daughter would act like a teenager again, and they would be at each other's throats. It got to the point where after her daughter's visits, the eighty-eight-year-old mother started having palpitations that lasted for two weeks. How on earth do you clean up a situation like that? Very carefully!

You might start by opening a conversation with your sibling like this: "Sis, you've been fighting a lot with Mom and it's affecting Mom's heart. I know she can be really hard to deal with, but I'm really scared that something bad could happen when you guys get into it. Please stop yourself from fighting with her."

Family Role Reversal: Are You Becoming the Parent?

If your sibling, is for any reason, unable or unwilling to have this type of conversation or respond to your request, you may have to approach your mother, father, family doctor, or most even-tempered and communicative sibling. In such a case, you might say, "Mom's been having palpitations after arguments with her, and I need your help." The complexities of effectively managing sibling relationships are dealt with in greater detail in Chapter 7.

By clarifying our gold standard of care, we know what we're striving for in this phase. But it's also important to acknowledge that having a gold standard is no guarantee things will go perfectly. There's an old adage that children are here to teach us that control is an illusion. Maybe our aging parents are here to teach us the same lesson. We may never be able to completely control all the elements of their lives as they age any more than they could completely control us when we were young.

And yet, that doesn't mean we've failed. Rather, we are becoming conscious of this phase of life, acquiring new tools, and striving to do our best. We are discovering how to make peace with ourselves, and if possible, how to help our parents do the same.

This Is Our Legacy

Our parents are not the only beneficiaries of our efforts. In a sense, the whole world is watching. As I write this, around ten thousand baby boomers are turning sixty-five each day.

Twenty-five percent of our population is aging within a culture that is fearful of getting old and dying. Their "SanGen" children are hopefully setting a higher standard of care for their families, their communities, and their nation.

We are the standard bearers for defining and creating the healthiest, most compassionate, and best kind of loving relationship between adult children and their aging parents. Just asking the question of what constitutes a gold standard of care opens up a conversation that families need to have. By becoming conscious of the way we are raising our aging parents and taking steps to become better sons and daughters, we are creating our family legacy—and our children are watching.

Chapter 3

What Your Parents Would Tell You, if Only They Could

One of the most powerful experiences we can have as human beings is the feeling of being understood. There is nothing quite like looking into the eyes of another person and seeing that they really get us. They listen to what we have to say and truly understand how we feel—no judgment, quick fixes, or unsolicited advice. Only their full, undivided attention.

Life may be filled with moments in which we feel utterly alone, but in that special, timeless moment, sitting across from someone who genuinely cares and who understands how we are feeling, we do *not* feel alone. Having someone in our life who is willing to walk in our shoes can and does make all the difference. "Compassion," it has been said, "is your pain in my heart." It can also be your joy in my heart. Do not underestimate the power of empathy when it comes to building intergenerational bridges. It is a gift like no other.

To feel seen, met, listened to, and understood is the basis for all loving relationships. And our ever-changing relationship with our aging parents is no exception.

Compassion is, of course, a two-way street. And "real-talk conversations," as I call them, where both people's feelings and needs are being communicated, are the lifeblood of healthy, vibrant AC/AP (adult child/aging parent) relationships. Many of us, however, did not grow up in families where we learned how to talk openly about how we felt or what we really wanted. Nor did our parents. Maybe there are a few things your parent would still like to tell you in a genuine, heart-to-heart talk. If so, what's holding them, or you, back?

They may not be willing or able to bring up an issue for a variety of reasons, starting with their being very private people, not being good communicators, or lacking confidence. Unaccustomed to being open and honest, they are adept at turning away from open-ended questions or inquiries as to how they really feel. Having mastered the art of small talk, some of our parents can meticulously avoid venturing into conversations that have an emotional charge. They probably don't spend a lot of time or energy sharing their thoughts and feelings—and don't want to burden us with "their" problems for fear it might scare us away.

But it's not always the parents who are uncomfortable with real talk. Adult children are equally guilty of small talk, changing the subject and side-stepping sensitive issues with deflection, sarcasm, and stonewalling.

What Your Parents Would Tell You, if Only They Could

Ben, a sixty-eight-year-old father of three, tried with little success to talk to his kids about his newly discovered heart problems.

"A few days after being told I needed stents, I called my kids," he told me. "I was very emotional and hoped I could talk to them without an 'Oh Dad, you're going to live forever' response. But that's what I got. Not one of them seemed to be willing or able to have a real conversation with me. I guess they're used to me being the dad. Well, I felt deeply disappointed and didn't say much more to my kids about the surgery. I decided to handle sensitive matters on my own from then on. Trouble is, my heart condition has gotten worse and I am going to need them more than ever. I probably should have said or done something a while ago, but I didn't. I need to talk with them now but I'm not sure where to start."

Your father or mother may, like Ben, initiate conversations with you. If not, it may fall on you and your siblings to initiate *real talk* with your parents. Whether you wait until issues arise in the middle of a crisis, or you bring things up proactively with your family, is up to you. Having worked with families for over forty years now and witnessed every kind of train wreck aging parents and their adult children can go through, I advise my clients to "stay ahead of the pain curve." Talking openly about family matters—be they legal, financial, logistical, or psychological—and working them out with civility, is the secret sauce for avoiding needless pain, stress, conflict, disharmony, and disaster.

> Talking openly about family matters—be they legal, financial, logistical, or psychological—and working them out with civility, is the secret sauce for avoiding needless pain, stress, conflict, disharmony, and disaster.

Here's another example: to crack the door on their eighty-year-old father's silence, address a few otherwise forbidden topics of conversation, and connect more deeply with their father, Susan and her sister, Geena, ages fifty-four and fifty-seven, took their father to lunch.

"Teaming up with Geena for this lovefest lunch with our dad at his favorite café was different than anything we had ever done," Susan told me. "We sat in a quiet corner of the café, asking him personal questions about his life. Our father did not stop talking, often tearfully, for several hours. He had never unburdened himself of feelings about his brother, mother, all of us children, his health, his career, and the greatest sources of joy and heartache in his life. Would this be a once-in-a-lifetime event? Or something that we would now get together and do whenever the time was right? Either way, it was something we will all remember forever."

My own mother was a good communicator. Over time, she learned that she could trust me with her innermost thoughts and feelings. Most of the time, all I had to do was ask and listen patiently. She'd tell me what she was going through, how she felt, and what she needed. Her openness was a blessing. I did not have to guess what was in my mother's heart as she got older. But this presented a great challenge for me as well. There were times when I wanted to run away from my mother's raw pain. At first, it was more than I knew how to handle. She was no longer the confident young mother who had dropped me off at elementary school and flew across the country to watch me defend my doctoral thesis. The days of picking her up and going to an opera or a play were ending. She had become the older, slower, weaker version of herself. And as her son, I had to recalibrate my expectations about what was still possible. With the passing of years, I learned to grieve the loss of who my mother had been, embrace who she had become, and enjoy what she was still capable of sharing with me. Listening to a close friend talk about his mother's inability to remember his name, I felt fortunate, and I learned to count my blessings.

My mom was also a pretty rare case in that she was so attuned to and insightful about her feelings so much of the time. And because of that, it was possible for me to talk openly with her and deepen our relationship. There were, of course, frustrating times when she was inwardly sad, hurt, angry, or upset; when she simply did not want to talk about it; and when she was losing an argument and would declare "case closed!" to end the discussion. My mother would later confess to feeling hurt, lonely, angry, or unhappy about something that had happened with one of her friends, family members, adult children or grandchildren. Or worse, she was grieving the loss of a close friend.

Then there are parents who are unable or unwilling to say how they feel, no matter how many questions you ask them or how good a listener you may be. A client of mine named Alyse is very worried about her seventy-five-year-old mom since her dad died six months ago. She feels helpless and frustrated to the point of not sleeping and getting stress headaches.

"Getting my mom to open up," she explained, "is like wringing blood from a stone. Without my dad, she's lost. I check in with her every day to see how she's doing. And if I'm lucky, I get something like, 'Eh, I'm okay.' Hey, I lost my father, and I'm grieving too. Please get me the new playbook for being a good daughter and not choking my mother to death."

Some parents are simply not accessible. Nor do they want to relinquish control. As one daughter put it, "My dad is going to hold on to the driver's seat for as long as it's humanly possible. This is his way of dealing with life at eighty-three, and I guess my job is to understand that."

We may not like it, but we need to know what we're working with. What kind of parent do I have? Are they somebody who is a communicator, willing to make adjustments and/or interested in being close to me? Or someone who is kicking and screaming as he gets older? In either case, it's likely that there are things they haven't yet told you—things they would tell you if they could or if they felt the moment was right . . . and where the power of understanding might open a few more doors of possibility.

What Your Parents Would Tell You, if Only They Could

They Would Tell You What Makes Their Hearts Sing

It's tempting to assume that the things our parents don't share with us all fall into the category of "negative" emotions that are too risky to share. After all, if it weren't unpleasant, why wouldn't they just share it? But mushy and happy feelings can be just as difficult—or even *more* difficult—to express than the unhappy ones. Softening their hearts and expressing affection might leave them feeling uncomfortably vulnerable. They might think it's too gushy. Or they might be afraid it won't be well received, that their kids will make a joke or say, "Come on, Dad; cut that out." They may be afraid, as so many of us are, that their show of affection will be met with discomfort by an adult child whose defenses are up.

When I wrote *The Secrets Men Keep*, I explored what I call "joking behavior," referring to the way men often express love and affection through sarcasm. At its core, this coded behavior is meant to dilute the closeness men often feel uncomfortable expressing.

An aging parent, or adult child, may feel similarly uncomfortable. Or they may feel okay with strong feelings but think their kids/parents won't be, so they hesitate to share. But what would an aging parent say if they felt truly at liberty? How would they act around us if they were less inhibited and fearful of being judged "a sentimental old hippie" or "an old nerd"?

Well, they would probably share with you the things that make their heart sing and those that make their heart heavy. This new season of life may have brought a whole slew of things that make them fearful and sad, or really happy and relieved. For instance, they may have resisted moving into a retirement community, but now they have found themselves surrounded by a new group of wonderful friends in a safe environment. They may be overjoyed, realizing that they haven't spent quality time with friends in many years. Or they may have lost their husband or wife, and recently they've met someone new with whom they're spending a lot of time, having a lot of fun, and feeling a surprising sense of companionship. Maybe they want to tell their kids all about it, but they're afraid of being judged or having their children feel protective of their deceased parent. Aging parents might not want to hear, "At your age, Dad?" or "Mom would be very jealous of her."

Perhaps an aging parent would confess that they're doing less and less every day, and that it actually feels good. They may have spent all last week doing nothing at all, and they loved it. Their nervous system may have been used for nonstop activity. Their whole lives may have been spent in a frenzy of productivity, and now, for the first time, they have the opportunity and space to relax—and it feels wonderful. They're rewiring their brain to a new way of being that's easier on their body, mind and spirit.

"My dad told me he is finally taking the time to do things he loves since retiring," one Courageous Aging workshop participant told me. "He loves his newfound freedom to just sit on the porch and read, go to a symphony, or go for a gentle hike. He's thinking about signing up for a Road Scholar trip to travel somewhere he and my mother have always wanted to go." Aging parents may be exploring ways they can volunteer, such as getting involved in community service trips organized by their synagogue or church. They might take the grandkids on a travel adventure that will surely become a lifetime memory or tutor high school students in their area of expertise.

Perhaps at this phase of their life, the littlest things are what makes their hearts sing. To them, the greatest gift may be as simple as a few minutes of quality time with you. There have been moments when I've wanted to tell my daughter that when she sees me with a goofy smile, all it means is that I'm loving the moment I have with her. Few things in my life have come close to the joy of just being with my daughters. And with two twin grandsons on the way, I cannot even imagine how much goofier my smile will become.

And They Would Tell You What Makes Their Heart Heavy

Of course, it's not just the happy things that our parents may have trouble telling us. For a whole host of reasons, they may be unable to share the things that are weighing heavily on their hearts. Some things seem too difficult to say out loud; our parent is simply embarrassed. Maybe they think they need to stay strong and set a "good" example for us no matter what. Or they want to save face. They don't want us to know how vulnerable and afraid they feel for fear we'll judge them, or maybe they just don't want to be pitied as "poor Dad" or "poor Mom," even for a second.

Another fear that aging parents often express is that of receiving unwelcome, unsolicited advice, in which we tell them how to manage this new and unknown life phase. They may be afraid we'll start making executive decisions against their wishes—a new residential setting, new medications, a new accountant or lawyer, or changes to the family business. We might render inaccurate, overly simplified interpretations of what they are going through and what they need and try to wrestle control from them.

But if only they could, they would probably like to confide in us the challenges this new phase of life has ushered in and the support they would welcome from us. Like most of us, they are likely experiencing a mix of emotions about the twists, turns, and transitions in their lives. They may be loving their newfound freedom—and yet, transitioning into retirement has likely been deeply difficult for them. Perhaps they don't have the identity they had before or that same sense of purpose. They may not feel they are making their contribution and engaging with the world. If they no longer enjoy the status they always had, that could be affecting their sense of self-worth. In fact, it may have negatively affected everything. They'll certainly have started to notice the way older people are often treated: like they're invisible. They don't want that to happen to them.

If they could, they might want to tell you what it's like to watch their own mind and body change right before their eyes. They can't remember things—certain words or the names of people they know—and it's a little scary. They can't do the

What Your Parents Would Tell You, if Only They Could

same things they always did. You might want to go out for eighteen holes of golf together, but they only feel up for nine at best. Maybe you used to go jogging together and they just can't anymore, and that makes their heart ache.

They might be afraid that, if they share these things, you will start walking on eggshells around them. They will start to be excluded from activities. They will become a burden and be left behind. And that worry only adds to the heaviness of their perceived loss of status and worth.

If they could, they might want to tell you what it's like to watch their friends pass away. They may have lost a handful of friends by this point, and they're starting to think about what it will be like to lose more of the people who are important to them—people with whom they share a lifetime of memories, like their husband, wife, little brother, older sister, or best friend of sixty years.

They might even want to tell you what it's like to seriously contemplate their own death. Indeed, they may at this moment be grappling with their impermanence for the first time, looking squarely at the mystery of what's next. They may be facing their mortality with the greatest faith they can muster and taking deep breaths. They may well be very scared of dying. At the same time, they may be starting to accept that the end of life is part of life, and, like the dying father of a close friend who asked his son to recite a beautiful, seven-century-old Rumi poem at his memorial service, feel a sense of peace at that thought.

In fact, many people harbor a greater fear of the decline that precedes death than of death itself. They are terrified of the losses they'll incur along the way, which are already happening. They don't want to lose their mind or for their body to fall apart, heading into such a downward spiral that all their money has to be spent on health care. Parents fear becoming a burden to their loved ones. And nobody wants to sit around like a lump while life goes on without them.

In the book *Younger Next Year*, authors Chris Crowley and Henry S. Lodge tell the story of an eighty-year-old man who loves to sail. He owns his own boat and scampers all over it like a much younger man. He even climbs right up the mainsail to make adjustments and repairs. One day he was up there at the top of the mainsail, banging around trying to fix something while a friend stood down below.

"You could slip off that thing and drown, and that could be it," said the friend. "Aren't you afraid?"

The man laughed.

"Yes, that's a possibility," he answered. "So what?"

For him, death was not the worst fate. He wasn't afraid of the end; what he feared was losing his vitality, his ability to spend his life doing the things he loved.

They May Be Afraid You Don't Want to Talk About It—and They May Be Right

Perhaps, as you've read the last several pages, you've felt sad because your mom or dad can't share these sorts of things with you. You might be asking why you didn't know certain things—the ways this new life phase could be a happy time for them, for instance, or the loss of self-worth that often accompanies retirement. And you may be wondering how it was that you and your parent co-conspired to remove such important things from the list of what you're "allowed" to talk about.

The truth is that we, as adult children, often don't want to talk about the deep challenges our parents are facing or the deep emotions they're feeling. We may not want to think about their life coming to an end. We might feel uncomfortable discussing strong feelings or anything even related to death. And they may sense our discomfort.

If yours is a family that has traditionally dealt with emotions or difficult feelings with jokes or sarcasm or avoidance, then you may have grown up to adopt this approach as your own. You didn't pick it, but it may be a part of you now. You may also feel resentment or frustration with your parent for helping to create that environment. They were at the helm of that avoidant culture, after all, and now it's affecting your family's ability to grow and change in this challenging time.

Of course, we can't change the way things went when we were growing up any more than we can change our parents. What we *can* do is acknowledge whatever role we've had up until this point in co-creating an atmosphere in which certain things were not admissible for discussion . . . and decide to make a change.

> If you would like to open a new kind of conversation with your parent, the most respectful way to begin is to ask for their permission.

If you would like to open a new kind of conversation with your parent, the most respectful way to begin is to ask for their permission. Say something as direct as, "Can we sit and talk about some of the challenges we're facing?"

By asking for permission, you're making yourself vulnerable first. And by framing it as a question, you are giving them permission to decline the conversation. That is their right, and there should be no punishment for them if they say no. This is an invitation that they are allowed to accept or decline, and they may need some time to think about it. You can always add that they can let you know when they are ready, and perhaps extend an invitation to have the conversation over coffee or lunch.

If they take you up on your offer, then you have an opportunity to create a judgment-free zone in which they can feel safe. In this zone your role isn't to figure things out and fix the problem or to offer unsolicited advice. It's not to make any assumptions about what you imagine is going on. It's just to be with them, to listen, to encourage, and to ask open-ended questions in the hopes of genuinely understanding what it's like for them.

"Get to know me!" one of my mother's friends at the retirement community told his twenty-one-year-old grandson, imploring the boy to put down his smartphone, open a line of communication by asking him a personal question, and begin to discover who he is.

Here's a Secret: Their Heart Sings When Their Children Understand

Your parent may or may not be willing or able to share anything about their inner lives and needs. But you'll have adjusted your approach. You've reoriented, even just slightly, toward showing them greater interest and understanding by really listening. This change effectively affords you a new range of possibilities. Now, when important issues are on the table, you are more likely to be able to understand the feelings involved and discuss them.

They will sense the difference. This shift will significantly increase your freedom to enjoy each other's company. In moments of family celebration, or private moments, you'll have more liberty to kick your heels up together and have fun. It's more likely that you and your parent will be able to let go, and to do so without the help of alcohol. Then you can both move a little closer to free expression of your love, playfulness, joy and curiosity.

You'll also be more capable of mobilizing in times of adversity, to come together to support each other when things get really difficult. That's because you have looked them in the eyes with a smile, assuring them of your love and willingness to listen, learn, love, and accept them. And in so being, in so doing, you've made their heart sing the songs of a lifetime.

If you would like to communicate even more effectively on sensitive topics with your parents, please visit my web site www.kendruck.com, where you will find articles, coaching tips and programs for moving forward.

Chapter 4

Caregiving Is a Two-Way Street

My uncle Irv loved to tell a story about the ninety-year-old woman who lived next door to his dental office. Every year, minutes after her seventy-year-old son's annual checkup, the mother would walk next door and ask my uncle, "How's he doing?"

In some ways our parents never stop being our caregivers. No matter how old they (and we) get, they will always be our parents. It's what they signed up for when we were born and it's often what they are most proud of in this life. That's why, even as we begin to assume responsibility for their care, it's important to acknowledge the exchange of love, support and caregiving to whatever extent is possible.

We moved my mother to a retirement community near my home in California in her early eighties. Her health had begun to decline and the cold New York winters had become a bit

> As we begin to assume responsibility for our parent's care, it's important to acknowledge the exchange of love, support, and caregiving to whatever extent is possible.

much for her. And while her children and grandchildren pitched in to make sure my mother had the loving care she deserved, as I mentioned earlier, it was also very important for all of us to make a point of asking my mother for her help.

She may not have been the mother and "Bubby" of old to her children and grandkids. But she was still our mother and grandmother, and she still had a wealth of love, affection, wisdom and lightheartedness to share with all of us.

On many occasions I would intentionally ask her for her help.

"Mom, can you help me think through something?"

"Mom, will you please read this and let me know what you think?"

She would gladly oblige by giving me her opinion. My decision to start writing the manuscript that became *Courageous Aging* was something my mother and I had discussed at length. Much as she had twenty, thirty, forty, fifty, and sixty years ago when I was a small boy, my mother's hands-on support and encouragement lifted me up. Once I began writing, I gave her chapters to read. She always had something to contribute about how people her age might react, and she provided a bolder, fresher perspective. And even if I couldn't

Caregiving Is a Two-Way Street

directly use her feedback, it was always a special way for us to connect.

My regular requests for her help and input had the effect of balancing out all the time I was now spending taking care of her. As we settled into our new roles, with me as her primary caregiver, there were plenty of times when both of us would talk about the way things used to be. Nothing can compare to the way a mother or father loves us. Nor can anything compare with the love of a son or daughter. When I would ask for my mother's help, it gave her another chance to show me her love, and it gave me the ability to benefit from the deep wisdom of her experience.

And just like the ninety-year-old mom asking about her elderly son's dental checkup, my mom remained attentive to my well-being until the very end. She was always concerned that I was working too hard, and she used to urge me to take better care of myself. She also never missed an opportunity to give me fashion advice when I'd invite her to join me at Men's Wearhouse!

Aside from occasionally wanting to prove I'd become a competent adult and getting defensive, my heart was warmed by my mother's care and attentiveness. When she would call me her "Zeese" and scratch my back the way she had done when I was a child, the little boy in me who was my mother's son came alive. I would reciprocate by reaching across to hold her hand in the car, at the symphony or at a holiday dinner. My mother would smile in that special way that told me she knew how very dear she was to me.

Ask for What They Can Give

Raising my two daughters taught me the importance of empowering our children and giving them responsibility. The logic of assigning household chores to kids isn't that they'll do the best job at washing the dishes, vacuuming the living room or doing their laundry. It's to give them the chance to learn that their contributions are meaningful and that they are a valuable part of the family. Cultivating this sense of responsibility takes effort and patience on the part of the parents. It will almost always be easier to do the dishes or vacuum the living room ourselves, but our kids won't feel responsible, or accountable, or independent if we always handle everything.

Might the same hold true with our aging parents? We don't want to create a completely dependent relationship.

"Don't worry, Dad, I'll take care of this for you. Don't worry, Mom, I've got it" is not the mantra to seek. Instead, in certain cases, you want to say, "Mom, Dad, I need your help. Will you please do this for me?"

You might be surprised to learn that a large percentage of aging parents come to think they have little or nothing to offer. They may be looking at you, in the prime of your life, with your career and your children and the added responsibility of taking care of them, and they may think that they're past the point of being able to help you. Seeing how much you're doing and how much weight you're carrying, they might welcome an opportunity to help in some way. But they don't want to burden you.

Caregiving Is a Two-Way Street

I can remember how exhausted and overwhelmed I felt when my staunchly independent mom's ability to fend for herself diminished to nothing. Our relationship had become very one-sided, and yet, there were still ways I needed my mother's help. I thought about what help she could still give, and then proceeded to occasionally ask for her advice, an hour of her time over lunch with her grandchildren, playing a song on the piano and her help in recording part of our family history on tape. As my grandchildren age, these will be some of the things my family and I will aim to teach them to keep them engaged with every member of the family and become a part of our activities.

Some parents are even in a position to help out financially or with watching the kids, and they are glad to be asked. Maybe you'd like to ask for something that would delight the child inside you, like getting a back scratch.

My close friend, Scott, petitioned his mother.

"Mom," he said, "will you take me out for a slice of rhubarb pie and vanilla ice cream on my birthday, like old times?"

Maybe some part of you would feel silly asking for that—and another part of you would absolutely love it. Or maybe it's something else, like telling your dad that you would like to inherit his wristwatch after he passes, and that you would like to be able to wear it as a reminder of him and how much you love him.

There are also some very practical legal and financial matters for which it may be appropriate, as well as necessary, to request their help. You may need them to sign estate planning or "what if" documents about their health and assets.

Though such requests can be met with resistance, as we'll explore in the next chapter, these issues don't necessarily have to turn into debates or arguments. In the context of a conversation about how they can reciprocate the help and care you're providing to them, you may find that they're more cooperative. It could be that they're capable of really listening to you and then helping you deal with the issues that need to be addressed.

Another practical area in which they may be able to help involves their stuff. As they downsize, family belongings that have accumulated over a lifetime will need to be stored, given away or even sold. Perhaps they're still living in the house that was your childhood home. In that case, decades' worth of personal effects from every family member may have piled up. When her father-in-law died, my friend Cindy found herself in the middle of a disaster.

"We had sixty-one years of living in that house to clean up and figure out what to do with," she said. "Who do you think is sorting through all these things?"

A couple of years ago a book came out called *The Gentle Art of Swedish Death Cleaning*, and it was sufficiently groundbreaking to attract the attention of *Time* magazine. While the name may strike some people as odd, the concept of "Swedish death cleaning" is that aging parents opt to clean and organize their own belongings so that their loved ones don't have to do it after they're gone. Leaving a legacy of love (not chaos), described in my book *Courageous Aging*, brings profound benefits that go far beyond cleanliness.

Maybe you ask your parent to do some of this cleaning and sorting with you, as an activity that brings you together. Going through family memorabilia, from pictures to old clothing, can be a deeply meaningful experience, an opportunity to remember shared history as well as to connect in the present moment. And, once their home is cleaned and reorganized, it will probably be a more pleasant and less stressful environment for them to live in. Asking for their help to begin this or some other process may be something that turns into a wonderful gift.

Here's another idea—but you have to remember, I'm from California, where we do weird stuff like this all the time! When my seventieth birthday came and went, my mom had already passed away, but I thought about what I would ask her for as a gift, if she were still alive. She loved to play the piano, and I had gotten a keyboard and headphones for her so she could play her music in her retirement home without disturbing her neighbors.

I think I would have asked her to play Mozart's "Rondo Alla Turca" for me—the way she had throughout my childhood—to celebrate that she was the one who had brought me into this world and who had done the work of helping to raise me into the man I have become. In addition to having her play the piano, I also would have asked her for Carvel ice cream. Why? Because she would have loved playing the piano and getting me a dip cone of Carvel (my father's favorite) for my birthday. Doing these things would have filled her heart. The idea is to ask for something that is within their means to give, and that perhaps only they can do for us.

Too often, we unconsciously yearn for something we did not get from our parents in childhood, and then mistakenly ask them for something they don't have the capacity to give. Simple requests become emotionally charged tests to determine whether or not our parents are finally going to satisfy the unmet needs of our childhood. And unsurprisingly, things unravel into hurt, anger, and chaos.

Testing our aging parent by asking for something they do not have the ability to give is a formula for disaster. And, it's something that should not even be considered without professional guidance of a qualified family counselor, coach, or therapist.

While there can be lots of love, fun, caregiving, and good conversation ahead, the days of our parents raising us are over. There's no such thing as a perfect parent, perfect child, or perfect childhood that's free of pain, disappointment and conflict. Having issues is just part of being human and growing up. Our sense of self-worth and lovability will, of course, still be affected by our relationship with our aging parents. My mother had the ability to occasionally reduce me to an eight-year-old with her sharp criticism—when I was in my sixties. But these matters are now in our hands. It's up to me to free myself of getting defensive when someone criticizes me, including my mother.

Caregiving Is a Two-Way Street

Parents who abuse or neglect their children, or who spent their adult years as "absent fathers and mothers," must, of course, be held accountable. Sometimes that means letting go of them and walking away. Other times, if they have proven themselves worthy of forgiveness, there is a path to parental redemption. Holding on to what happened, or did not happen, back then is our decision. We can find the strength to accept that they did the best they could with what they had and live with those limitations. We can spend our days vengefully punishing them for their transgressions or search for ways to make peace with what happened and go on purposefully with our lives.

If and when you do ask for something from your parents, make it something that is meaningful and attainable. Depending on how you think it might be received, present them with a short list of how you need their help.

"I came up with a few ideas for how I need your help," you might say, and then give them the list. Whether or not they take you up on any of your ideas is up to them. Explain that you will not love them one ounce less if none of the things on your list actually happen. It's a bit like buying someone a houseplant; you never ask how the plant is doing. They might have killed the plant, so don't ask. By suggesting that they help you, you're creating an opportunity that can in itself be a gift.

When Caregiving Is a One-Way Street

When a parent truly may not have the capacity or the willingness to give back to us, and the caregiving runs in only one direction, we have a choice. We can make the sacrifices that come with taking care of our parent and reset our expectations about getting anything in return. Coming to terms with the limitations of our situation and doing our best to be good sons and daughters while taking care of ourselves might be the smart choice. Or, we could either go through the motions of caregiving with underlying feelings of anger and resentment or walk out the door and abdicate responsibility for the care of our parent. When caregiving is a one-way street, it's a difficult but consequential choice to make.

Brainwashed to believe that "selfish" is always a bad thing, some adult children have great difficulty in taking care of their own needs when caring for an aging parent. They believe that they must, after all, be selfish, self-involved, ungrateful and unloving sons or daughters for considering their own needs as well.

When we buy into the idea that self-care is selfish, we come to believe that it's shameful simply to say and do what we need to in order to feel okay. This is so wrong. Good or healthy "selfishness" is about having the courage and strength to do the right thing for ourselves. We must recognize what it will take to feel good about ourselves, acknowledging that it is absolutely okay—and, in fact, essential—for us to say and do the things that will allow us to take care of our own health and sanity, and to be at peace.

In a perfect world, our aging parents would be aware of the pressures we're under, the things weighing most heavily on

Caregiving Is a Two-Way Street

our hearts, the power they have to reduce stress in our lives, and the ways they can help us. But the world is not perfect. Sadly, some of our aging parents have become so self-involved that they are oblivious to our lives and our needs. We are not going to get the kind of attention from our parents that we need, though it may be what we have craved throughout our whole lives. So we need to let go and do what's "next best."

Next best is the bargain we strike with ourselves to do what we can and let go of what we cannot control. It means taking the time to pat ourselves on the back for being a good son or daughter, appreciating all that we have done and doing the best we can. We then take responsibility for getting some of our own needs met. That often means saying "no" to doing more and saying "yes" to doing less—including unplugging from a schedule of nonstop activity to take a bath, play soothing music, go for a walk, get a massage, see a therapist, or escape to a movie.

Searching for Balance

The question of how to balance care for ourselves with care for our parents is not an easy one, and there is no perfect answer. The unpleasant truth is that some decisions in this life will be uncomfortable no matter what we do; no matter which alternative we choose, there will be a downside, and we won't feel entirely at peace.

I remember years ago, as I came to terms with the painful decision to end my marriage, I never felt 100 percent certain that it was the right decision. After many years of counseling and consternation, 85 percent of me knew my wife and I were headed on different paths, and that it was not in our best interests to stay married. But I kept waiting and wanting to become 100 percent sure. At times I felt more certain than others—but then I would have moments of doubt where I could not imagine being apart from my wife of twenty-six years. I never did reach being 100 percent certain, and slowly learned that some things in life are never going to be 100 percent one way or another.

Each of us must decide how to balance our own needs with the needs of our parents, and it's likely that we'll never be completely certain that we've done the right thing or that we have done enough. An occasional surge of doubt and discomfort will arise as some part of us argues that we chose wrong. Whether it's a decision we make about our marriage, kids, our parents, pets, or ourselves, this second-guessing may continue.

After I lost my mother, I had moments of doubting the decision to move her into a retirement community instead of into my own home. Was that the right thing to do? Could I have been a more loving, diligent son? She said that she loved the people in her community, she had her doctor right there, she had a swimming pool, and she was part of a social group. But was it really the best thing? Was it truly best-case scenario for her?

When such doubts arise, and I am invited into the torture chamber of guilt, I remind myself that I made the best decision

Caregiving Is a Two-Way Street

that I could make at that time. I did the best I could with what I knew in that moment. Though I may never feel completely certain about every one of the decisions I made, I can put up a stop sign in front of the door to that torture chamber and make peace with how things turned out.

Much of this journey of raising an aging parent is about reflection and deliberation—the process of finding out what we need to do in order to know we've done our best. There will always be times of questioning and doubt, when we confront yet another new situation with our parent and don't know how to position ourselves. As each new situation arises, we are striving to make good choices and do the right thing, whether or not it's the hardest way forward.

The fact that we are striving to be okay with ourselves and be there in a loving way for our parents is critically important. That sense of inner peace is crucial for all of us, and it will be especially relevant where we're heading next. In the next two chapters, we will cover some of the most common yet difficult conflicts that arise while raising an aging parent: resistance from parents who fight change and reject our efforts to help, and the sibling rivalries that so often resurface at the very same time.

Chapter 5

"I'll Never Give Up My Car Keys!" — When Parents Resist Change

Most of us don't think about what aging will truly look and feel like until we're faced with the reality of it. This may have been the case with your parents. Perhaps, at the end of their career, they had a glorious retirement party and received glowing accolades from a lifetime's worth of adoring colleagues. Maybe that retirement party was a pinnacle for them—a moment when everyone in their life came together to remind them how much they had achieved and what a difference they'd made in their office, their business, or their field at large. Maybe they were elated and set their sight on exciting new horizons, or maybe they woke up the next morning staring into an abyss and grieving the loss of their primary source of meaning and purpose.

Their entire life and identity may well have revolved around their work, which was their contribution to the world. And then they felt—in what may have been an abrupt change—that they had aged out and become a has-been. Change is difficult for pretty much everyone, and a change of that magnitude can be difficult beyond measure.

Or they may have faded quietly back into the woodwork of a simple, unremarkable life after retiring. No retirement party. No accolades. No real sense of having contributed anything extraordinary, or of having left their mark with the work they did. Maintaining this low profile into life's post-work season may leave them feeling at peace—or empty, wondering what it was all for.

The truth is that we all love our comfort zones. And we crave familiarity, predictability, and certainty. The problem is that we live in a world that's constantly changing. In his epic song, "Everything Changes," my dear friend, singer-songwriter Mark Spiro, who brilliantly produces my audiobooks, reminds us that "Everything changes under the setting sun. So will we."

At this instant, the daylight is changing, the season is changing, our bodies are changing, and everyone and everything we know is changing around us. It's hard for us to grasp that reality—never mind face its implications for our own lives as we get older.

And the same is true for our parents. While some parents may be better than others at rolling with the punches, this later-life phase is to some degree destabilizing for nearly everyone. After a lifetime of work, family and, hopefully, good physical health, most of our parents feel pushed out of their aging comfort zone once again. Between having to remake themselves and their lives yet again, and grappling with perhaps the most difficult transition they have ever confronted, it is not surprising that they may want to clench their fists, dig in their heels, and resist.

"I Don't Want to Talk About It"

Gradually, you may have started to feel concerned about your parent engaging in activities that seem risky, unwise, negligent, or even dangerous. Driving, especially at night, is a common example. Another is choosing to remain in their own home when it seems that they can no longer safely take care of themselves. And yet another, which can appear in various forms, is the way they choose to take care of—or disregard—their own health. You may have felt uncomfortable for a long time before deciding to raise the issue with them—and then you found yourself stonewalled.

"I don't want to talk about it," they tell you. Or maybe they insist, "I've got it handled."

They may also lash out, perhaps accusing you of sounding like a nagging spouse. "You sound like your mother," your father might say, or vice versa. Perhaps they received years of needling on the same or similar issue from a spouse who is no longer living, and they are resolute in not wanting to hear it from you. It can be confounding when Mom or Dad denies having taken double doses of a potentially fatal heart med, stepped on the gas instead of the brakes and plowed into the garage, or made their third trip to the ER this year after fainting.

Alternatively, either your mom or dad may be acting as an enabler for the other. Maybe you dad had a near-fatal heart attack and came home from the hospital with detailed instructions about what to eat and how much to exercise. And maybe your mom acts like she never saw or heard a word of it. "What would you like to eat tonight?" she asks, and keeps on preparing his favorite pastas. Or she thwarts his suggestion to go for a walk, proclaiming, "You're tired, it's been a long day."

Sometimes the enabler is a caregiver who is even more stubborn than the parent who is grappling with a needed change.

"Stay out of this!" he or she will say. "You don't know what he needs. I've been taking care of him all along: I know what he needs." Dealing with a parent who has been enabling the other for fifty years—and finding yourself in the unenviable position of having to intervene—can be difficult if not treacherous.

Our parents may use every trick in the book to avoid looking at the issue that needs attention. They don't want to give up their car keys even if they have a sense that continuing to drive is unsafe. They don't want to give up their home even if they're aware that their living situation (walking up a flight of stairs, cleaning, taking care of the family pet, etc.) has become untenable. They don't want to deal with grave health issues because it may mean giving up certain things—foods, beverages, behaviors, a sense of self—to which they feel a strong attachment.

In order to avoid facing these uncomfortable circumstances, then, parents are doing more than just avoiding the conversation with you. They may be trying to hide what's going on. They may be in denial. They may be self-medicating, numbing themselves in order to escape having to think about or do anything. Or they may have fallen into a clinical depression and need help.

But the cost of avoiding, or enabling, has finally grown too high. The issues are now affecting the whole family.

The debt on avoidance has come due.

A New Agreement
There is nothing easy about the situation created by avoidance. Take a moment to acknowledge how hard this is and to recognize your own desire to be a good son or daughter with the threat of conflict looming. Remaining strong yet humble at those times in life when we're being called to be both forceful and compassionate is always wise.

Sometimes we simply need to step back and take a moment or two to perform a reality check with a sibling, close friend, or someone we trust to make sure what we've decided about taking care of our parents is proportionate to the reality of the situation. Respectful. Justifiable. And necessary. Thinking through and deciding on the best course of action takes time, courage, faith, and lots of good research. It also involves stepping back and making sure that we're not overreacting.

Hovering over an aging parent when they're perfectly capable of handling the situation is as counterproductive as doing the same thing with your children when they are small. Treating someone as helpless when they're capable of participating to some degree or another in the decisions of their own lives is disempowering, humiliating, and corrosive to any relationship.

In the 2018 movie *Book Club*, Diane Keaton rightfully calls out her adult daughters for trying to control her life several years after her husband—their father—passed away. Infuriated by her daughter's age-biased admonition, Keaton's character responds, "It's time for all of this to just stop! You have very strong parenting instincts but save it for your own children. I know I am getting older, but I'm doing just fine." She then packs up her things and moves out of her daughter's home, assuring her adult children that she's not only perfectly capable of managing her life, she also has things she wants to explore, including a new relationship.

> Always make sure you're not disempowering and or humiliating your mother or father when they are still capable, to any degree, of deciding their own future.

There will undoubtedly be tough times when it's necessary for some of us to step up and take charge of our parents' lives, and it will be the right thing to do. But you will always want to make sure you're not disempowering and or humiliating your mother or father when they are still capable, to any degree, of deciding their own future. Taking the reins when they are no longer capable is

When Parents Resist Change

one thing. Overreacting, making executive decisions for them, and wrestling control from them is another.

If your parent won't, or can't, talk about changes that are necessary for their health or safety, if they're unwilling or unable to take responsibility for themselves, you or someone in your family—even their doctor, or people in their community—will probably need to step up. To do this effectively, you'll need to get clear about the terms and conditions of your involvement.

Well-thought-out agreements about what your role is going to be, as well as what role others in the family will play, are the best assurance your collective attempts to intervene will produce good results. Once again, it is critical to communicate your intentions in a soft but firm tone—including your concerns, goals, intentions, and willingness to spend time and money and to advocate for them—and then follow through with action.

Parents who know that you, and your family, and good people in their community care and want to help them maintain good health, have a safe and comfortable place to live, get the medical attention they need, see their grandchildren, and find meaning and purpose in each day are very fortunate. But these things are best achieved in partnership.

Next, we need to tell them what we need from them in order for us to be successful. For example, we need them to listen to what we're saying, keep an open mind, share their concerns, have faith in us, and give us their trust. Whether that means moving, agreeing to see a doctor, signing papers, no longer driving at night or something else, we need to tell them how they can help us help them. We might even want to lay it all out clearly by writing it down. This way, everyone is in agreement and operating together.

Finally, we need to make changes known to caregivers, doctors, lawyers, our siblings, and anyone else who is involved. Siblings who have not been included in the decision-making process may show up on the scene and effectively undermine the progress we've made with our parents. Storming in as family heroes and rescuers, and accusing us of cheating, upsetting or mistreating a parent with unwarranted criticism may be a reckless attempt to satisfy a long-held sibling rivalry, but it has the power to reduce your work into a proverbial train wreck.

That's why it's important to consider proactively telling your siblings about any new agreements you're entering into with Mom or Dad. Explain the situation in a non-adversarial tone, and do your best to get your siblings' buy-in for this change. You want and need their support if possible.

Stepping back and unplugging from high drama involving our parents and siblings, especially if our family of origin is prone to drama, can be difficult. But it is essential to our health and well-being and that of our parents.

My friend Susan did a "step back" when her older sister called at 7:00 a.m. from the intensive care unit of the local hospital. Their seventy-four-year-old mother, who had become a drama queen in recent years, had driven herself to the hospital fearing she was having a heart attack.

When Parents Resist Change

"Something's happening to Mom, and you need to get here right away!" Susan's sister insisted.

Having lost their younger sister to drug addiction several years earlier, Susan and her family knew what it was like to live through a tragedy. They had all blamed themselves for the sister's death. But Susan and her sister were also keenly aware that their mother had become a hypochondriac.

They had spoken to her very lovingly about not panicking or "crying wolf" at the smallest sign of a health problem. And they had emphatically asked her to go in for regular checkups, see a therapist to reduce her anxiety, and become more proactive in dealing with her health by exercising and eating healthy foods.

After speaking to her mother's physician at the ICU, Susan decided not to rush to the hospital.

"I'm so proud of myself, Ken," she told me. "I'm tired of running around with my hair on fire, responding to my mother's latest false alarm and call for attention. Though her doctor assured me she was probably having another anxiety attack, I know that something might go terribly wrong in the ICU with my mother—that she, like my sister, could die—and I will not have been there with her. But I can't live in fear of my mother, or anybody I love, dying. And I can no longer torment myself with guilt that I could or should have been there to save someone's life, like I did with my sister."

We strike a life-changing bargain with ourselves when we decide to step back and resist a family member's seductive invitations to drama, knowing that something bad might happen. We agree to live with what we decide is the best we can do at the time, and we refrain from mercilessly second-guessing ourselves. We also accept the fact that despite all our finely crafted coping skills and abilities, we will, at times, be defenseless against our own guilt and sorrow. We need to take a deep breath and try our best to just let it go.

Tools for a Successful Intervention

Of course, convincing a resistant parent, like Susan's, to make changes and accept help is much easier said than done. It may require a great deal of creativity and persistence, as well as a stronger, more loving tone; greater amounts of patience; and a clear, well-thought-out plan. How can we best engage with this difficult situation and a stubbornly resistant parent? An effective intervention may have to involve bringing our parent's trusted family physician, clergy, lawyer, relative or close friend into the conversation.

Remember when your kids were small, and it took an uncle or a neighbor to get through to them about eating their vegetables? It may be necessary to reach out to the folks our aging parents listen to and trust, to get their full attention. From experience, I know that getting my mom's doctor involved in the conversation about trying a medication to quell her anxiety resulted in a breakthrough.

Some adult children report that they reached a resistive parent by writing them a heartfelt letter—telling them how much they love them, how concerned they are for their well-being, and imploring them to consider a change. Maybe such a letter can take them step by step into the opportunity side of their situation and explain that we are doing nothing which would put them at risk. Or perhaps it would be best to get their grandchildren involved. Maybe the parent has an especially strong relationship with one of their grandkids, and hearing concerns voiced by the younger generation would prove most effective.

Whatever the particular strategy we choose, the idea is to do some careful thinking about the approach we believe will be most effective with our parent. What might they need to hear from us or someone they trust in order to consider making a needed change? What must we do to best tailor our strategy to who they are and what they need? What can we do so they feel enough of a sense of love, support, trust and respect that they let go?

What If They Say No?
Do any of the following statements sound familiar?
"That's not what I want."
"Your sister's helping us."
"I didn't ask for this."
"I'm going to keep driving."
"I'm not moving."
"I refuse to go to a doctor and if you don't like it, that's too effing bad."

Our parent may flat-out reject our willingness to get involved, and our request for change. They may insist that they're going to continue to engage in behavior that we recognize is unsafe. At this point, similar to what some of us did when our kids exercised poor judgment, we can choose to resort to more serious "tough love"-type approaches. These can be anything from escalating the intensity of your request into an authoritative demand (something that is extremely awkward and uncomfortable to do with the primary authority figure in your life) to hosting an all-in family intervention with others who are supportive of the change including your other parent, brothers, sisters, aunts, uncles, and grandchildren, trusted doctor, or attorney.

For instance, if they refuse to give up driving, and we're clear that driving is too dangerous, but they defiantly tell us they're going to keep on driving—we must consider setting limits for them. Telling your mother or father that you are taking over their decision-making might sound something like this:

"Dad, I love you, but I can't stand by and let you continue driving. I thought of telling you, 'Don't call me if you get into an accident or there's some other kind of problem. I will not be there to make excuses for you.' But I can't take that risk. I love you too much to stand by and watch you endanger yourself and others."

We acknowledge that they may be so angry with us for saying this that they may want to tell us to go jump in a lake. They may even feel like they never want to speak to us again.

When Parents Resist Change

We can give them an example of how someone like them benefitted from a needed change and explain that it is our hope and prayer that they will see us as trying to prevent them from having to go through something truly horrible.

In some cases, tough love will crack open a door to new possibilities. Maybe it will lead to a conversation about consulting a higher authority, such as their doctor, lawyer, or minister. Or perhaps it will lead to our handing them a one-hundred-dollar gift certificate to Uber or Lyft, so they won't need to drive. Advances in technology, like easy-to-use smartphones, and tech-friendly services, like GoGo Grandparent, make it easy for aging parents and grandparents to arrange affordable transportation. Whatever the solution, sometimes it takes newfound strength for you to have these hard conversations—and, in some cases, endure a painful period of silence in order to get there.

In one family I worked with, the most difficult conflict revolved around the father's behavior at his retirement home. He was sneaking out of his room at night and climbing into bed with the eighty-two-year-old woman next door. This was strictly prohibited in the facility and, at least in this case, that rule was for a good reason: it wasn't clear that the woman in the next room had the cognitive capacity to consent to a male visitor. Despite warnings, the father continued to leave his room at night to go next door.

Eventually, his son got a call saying his dad was about to get thrown out of the facility, and he rushed over.

"Dad, you cannot go into this woman's room. You absolutely cannot do this anymore. If you get thrown out, we will be forced to find a single-sex facility with locked doors. Is that what you want? That is your alternative: When you go to bed at night, the door will be locked. It's your choice."

In no uncertain terms, we must lay out the consequences of our parent's actions. The next move is theirs, and we hope they can make it wisely.

When the Interventions Don't Work

There may come a moment when we realize that we've done everything we can and that further efforts and attempts to convince them will get us nowhere. We've tried every strategy, and the parent continues to refuse our help. At this point, we know in our heart that we have done all that we can to shield them and to elicit their cooperation.

And now we have to follow through with the tough-love consequences that we laid out for them. In the case of the father who went into his neighbor's room at night, the message became, "Dad, in spite of what we talked about and what you assured me you would no longer do, you keep going in her room. There's nothing I can do now. You can no longer live here."

In some cases, we reach an impasse and have to step back completely. There's nothing else we can possibly do. Left with declarations such as, "I can't take any further responsibility for your driving," or ". . . for you continuing to live on your own," we must face several challenges, the first of which is our own powerlessness. We realize that we are not going to be able to control or influence our parent's situation. We may blame ourselves for failing to do what was necessary to save, help, or protect our parent. And we grieve this loss, searching for some measure of peace and assurance that we did our best to improve a truly difficult situation. Seeking refuge and struggling to turn our attention toward living the other, more hopeful parts of our life, we may lapse back into sorrow. Replaying what happened, we still search for answers, words, and creative solutions but to little or no avail.

Peace of mind may be elusive, if not impossible at this time. But we must summon the faith, strength, and courage to accept what is and move forward.

If They Choose to Accept Our Help

Sometimes, after stepping back, we catch a break, and our parent will agree to take our suggestion. This doesn't necessarily happen immediately, or even quickly, but they may eventually decide that there's some wisdom in what we or one of their trusted confidantes have been telling them. Now what?

We take this moment to share how relieved we are that they're now willing to make some changes. And accept our help.

"Thank you, Mom," we might say. "After all you've done for me, the hundreds of thousands of times you've shown up for me or asked me to do something that was in my best interest, for you to accept my help now means the world to me."

We acknowledge their trust and willingness to make a change that is so difficult. Then we start putting the plan for change into action.

We can expect to do some hand-holding at this stage of the process, as they will likely need help making the change. When this happens, we must pause every so often and ask them how things are going, how they are feeling, and whether there are any further adjustments that need to be made.

And just because they've agreed to change doesn't always mean it will be smooth sailing from there on out. There may be some sharp turns in the road, obstacles and roadblocks of fear and resistance. We must see our parents trying, in their own way, to deliver on their agreement. Encourage them. Help them take bold new steps in their life, much the way they might have done for us as children. We must make it safe for them to feel vulnerable, with assurances like, "How could someone who just moved from their family home of sixty years, and who lost their beloved wife, not feel a little lost? Please give yourself some time. I'm right here with you, Dad."

No Matter What, We Give Away the Full Measure of Our Love

Our parents will do the best they can. So will we. Our expression of gratitude need not be limited to thanking our parents for their cooperation. Indeed, they may not be able to accept our help or cooperate at all. Yet it is still important that we acknowledge their best efforts, rather than abandon or punish them when all is said and done.

I chose to celebrate Valentine's Day one year by creating my own card covered in little red hearts, and listing "25 Things I Love About You" for my mother. Of course, I didn't mention the one hundred things about her that drove me crazy! Reading all those particular things that I loved meant the world to her. She put the card on her dresser and treasured it for the rest of her life.

> Parents will do the best they can and it is important that we acknowledge their best efforts, rather than abandon or punish them when all is said and done.

In really difficult times, accessing feelings of love for our parents can be difficult. In those moments, though, we can search our memories for specific things that soften our hearts to remember. And we can share those things with our parent as peace offerings:

"The show tunes, symphonies and operas you played for us as children on weekend mornings."

"The time you held our dad, telling him how much we loved him."

"That time you got up in the middle of the night and put Vicks VapoRub on my chest." "Your hokey, pokey and lokey jokes, and love of Carvel ice cream, Dad."

Raising an aging parent is, above everything else, about giving away the full measure of our love. Whatever love we feel, we give away. Sure, we acknowledge the hardship and pain that comes with growing up; we don't deny any of it. And we all have issues with our parents that can last a lifetime. And yet, at the same time, we humbly allow ourselves to feel the love we have for our parent. And we make sure they receive that love while we still have the chance to share it with them.

Chapter 6

"Mom Always Liked You Best!" — When Sibling Rivalries Resurface

As soon as my wife became pregnant with our second child, we began explaining the news to our daughter Jenna. Preparing Jenna for the enormous change of having a baby sister was a fun challenge for a young psychologist. Our daughter had become the center of our universe, and we went out and bought every book on the subject to teach us how to talk to her about the little baby that was about to join our family. With Jenna in our laps, or while tucking her into bed, or while sitting together at dinner together, we talked with her about the joys and responsibilities of being a big sister. And we added picture books that told the story of a new baby's arrival. We also included Jenna in our preparations, inviting her to help us get the baby's room ready, pick out cute little stuffed animals, and talk to the baby when it was moving "in Mommy's tummy."

With each step, we brought Jenna into the fold, doing everything possible to prepare our beloved little girl for the arrival of her baby sister. Fearing that having to share her parents might be a cataclysmic, unwelcome change for Jenna and that she would feel she would no longer be the center of our universe, we did everything we could. My wife and I were pretty sure we had nailed it, and then Stefie was born.

Wheeling my wife out of the hospital with little Stefie in her arms, it was time for Jenna to meet her baby sister. "Come and meet Stefie, sweetheart," we said, glowingly.

Jenna came right up and kissed Stefie on the forehead. And . . . that was it.

"Okay," she said, "can we go home now?"

The way Jenna saw it, it was time to head back to our house and leave this little person at the hospital where she belonged. Apparently, we had forgotten to mention that the baby was coming home with us! Forever. Jenna was stunned. Could this be true? Was she really no longer going to be the center of our universe?

Rivalry Is Universal

Sibling rivalry is part of human nature, and our sisters and brothers become our first rivals. Robert Fulghum's famous book *All I Really Need to Know I Learned in Kindergarten* makes a case for the simple and important life lessons that we learn when we first go to school, but for most of us, that learning begins even earlier, with our brothers and sisters. It is thanks to our brothers and sisters that we first develop a sense of life as, in part, a competition, as Jenna did. And it is our siblings from whom we hopefully, eventually learn how to play nice, how to share, and maybe even how to trust.

> It is our siblings from whom we hopefully, eventually learn how to play nice, how to share, and maybe even how to trust.

Brothers and sisters can be one of life's greatest blessings. The longest relationships we have are often the ones we have with our siblings. The experiences we share and closeness we have with a beloved brother and/or sister are often immeasurable. But getting along with our siblings can also be one of life's greatest challenges and sources of conflict.

We sometimes idealize the concept of family—family dinners, family celebrations, trips home for the holidays. And it's true that our families of origin can be sources of profound love as well as fun and fond memories. But we're also talking about a group of people who were squeezed into a house together and expected to function as a cohesive unit. Where there are siblings, there are pretty much always sibling rivalries. The question, then, isn't whether there's tension, jealousy, and competition for our parents' love and attention, but how those things are handled.

Siblings who allowed their conflicts and differences to surface while still living in the family home together have stories and scars that bear testimony. And those whose feelings are rarely if ever allowed to surface get older and push off into the world with unresolved business that may fade into the background as they go about their own lives.

Our brothers and sisters, and the unresolved conflicts and rivalries of childhood, are no longer right in our faces; we have some breathing room, so resolving those issues tends to slide down on our list of priorities. Eventually, we have our own families and they become the focus of our attention.

But if anything can reactivate dormant family conflicts, it's our parents growing older and requiring care. That's why we can't have a complete conversation about raising an aging parent without talking about the issues that are likely to arise between brothers and sisters.

When the parent/child roles begin to reverse, and the caregiving needs of an aging parent arise, some of the old and problematic rivalries and family dynamics can come roaring back. Who is going to step up and take care of Mom and Dad? Who has been the good son or daughter all these years? Who can Mom and Dad turn to and trust? Who is unreliable and untrustworthy? Who's the family hero? The family slug? It all comes bubbling up to the surface.

At the call for help of an aging parent, it becomes clear which of their children seem to be stuck in the psychology of their childhood, playing out time-worn jealousies, conflicts, trauma, and resentments, and who has risen above those issues, is capable of providing care to their parents, and may now be ready to let go of the past, show up, and pitch in.

Conflict Comes in Every Shape and Size

It has been said that all of our families are uniquely dysfunctional, and that every sibling will have their own unique challenges when it comes to dealing with their parents. For the past thirty years, I've conducted family council meetings with every imaginable kind of family. In almost every instance, the challenges of at-risk families were faced down by family members moving to another level of understanding, communication, forgiveness, humility, and compassion.

In one family of five, a thirty-five-year-old brother had been dubbed the problem child by his father, brothers, and sister because of his penchant for gambling. In the view of his siblings, their mother was acting as his enabler. Her problem son had scarcely worked a day in his life, but she repeatedly relegated everything and everyone else in her life to second priority in order to help get her son out of trouble. Eventually, she even funded his move from New York down to Florida, where she lived, because he had loan sharks after him.

Despite the protests of her family, the mom was never willing to consider doing anything but bail him out, even though, for her, he was a constant source of acute anxiety. As she aged, her anxiety morphed into heart disease. As the other two siblings took care of the mother, the problem son would make a token visit once a month, which upset the mother to the point of it compromising her already failing health. The other siblings begged her to stop enabling their brother, but she would have none of it.

Then there's the case of a bicoastal family in which the aging parent lived in Santa Barbara near one of the kids, while the other kid lived on the other side of the country, in Connecticut. The nearby sibling managed the mother's care on a day-to-day basis—but the distant sibling only made bimonthly visits, motivated in part by the guilt she felt for being so far away.

When this faraway sibling came to town she would pick up her mother and take her to see new doctors, thereby disrupting the continuity of care the mother was receiving from her existing team. New doctors would issue new orders, and Mom's care became a confusing hot mess. Mired in their own conflict, with one begging the other not to undermine the standing plan for the mother's care, the siblings were soon at each other's throats.

What if there's also a family business involved? For years, I have specialized in working with families who own and operate a business together, the dynamics of which can be both incredibly rewarding. And incredibly thorny.

In one such case, an aging father, who was the business owner and family patriarch, began to feel threatened by his eldest son, who had graduated from a top business school with an MBA and worked for eight years for a Fortune 500 company, attaining a top management position. Although his sister and younger brother also worked in the family business, this son was clearly his father's intellectual and business equal. Unlike his siblings, who felt obligated to follow their dad's orders, he called out his father when he was wrong and/or when he was in danger of steering the ship off course.

But Dad, who seemed to be falling further and further behind in his understanding of how their business was changing, quietly saw these confrontations as an insult to his leadership. His response was to passive-aggressively discredit his son. He slowly and quietly stripped him of authority and embarrassed him in front of colleagues and siblings, who stood by and allowed it to happen. As his siblings continued to enable their father, their mother became increasingly fearful of her family breaking apart and spoke up.

After getting my name from a close friend, she called me for help, and I met with the entire family. As I started working with them, it became clear that there was a longstanding problem in the family dynamic. The older son, once hopeful of succeeding his father, was heartbroken about not being able to continue working with his family and felt he had no choice but to resign. His departure was not only unfortunate for the family, it also was devastating for the business. It took months of intensive family meetings for his father and siblings to admit they had turned their backs on him and had recklessly hurt the business in the process. Their family began a long healing process and a succession-planning exercise, both of which continues to this day.

Family dynamics are very powerful. They can become the focus of our insights and awareness, or reside just beyond our awareness in our subconscious. Sorting out the issues in this particular family was akin to performing brain surgery because the dynamics were so far out of most everyone's awareness as to make them unreachable.

> Family dynamics are very powerful. They can become the focus of our insights and awareness, or reside just beyond our awareness in our subconscious.

It doesn't take a family business, a complicated power dynamic with a patriarch, or a child becoming either a superstar or a "problem" to sow a deep conflict amongst siblings and parents. In fact, the root of a deep conflict can be as simple as one sibling performing just a little better than the others and gaining status in his parent's eyes.

One sibling is more financially successful; one sibling has a happy marriage while the other doesn't. One sibling has kids who are going to college and seem to be on their way to having productive lives, while the other grandchildren are struggling. Any of these situations can fester and cause difficulty. Or perhaps one sibling has always had the nagging sense that Mom likes the other sibling better. Sadly, that's all it takes to trigger a crisis and throw a brother–sister relationship into chaos.

A Chance to Take Inventory and Humble Ourselves

There came a point in my own journey when I realized that I had not been the easiest person for my own brother and sister to grow up with. In some ways I had, in fact, been extremely challenging for them. I became only more challenging as an adult, in particular, after my daughter, Jenna died. When I lost her, I felt completely destroyed. To my siblings, I was inconsolable and unreachable.

When Sibling Rivalries Resurface

Years later, when our mom began to require more care, many of our family issues came to the surface. Addressing my differences with my brother and sister meant taking inventory of myself.

"What was it like to have Ken Druck as a brother?" I asked myself.

"Not easy."

I used this time as an opportunity to consider how broken I was, how I had rendered myself unapproachable, and the ways that my devastating loss had affected my whole family. I also had to own up to the ways that my successes in rising up from despair had won me "favored son" status with my mother, and how hard that might have been on my brother and sister. It made me wonder how many of us are driven to success—proving, pleasing, overachieving, enabling, or struggling as a way of winning the battle for status with our parent.

I recently had the opportunity to interview a famous sports psychologist who was working with a professional golfer. He said that this golfer had an incredible wife—a person who really understood what it meant to be married to a superstar. To be sure, it's no easy task to be married to a star, someone who is always achieving the next great thing, and who is constantly in demand and receiving praise and accolades from others. It takes a very special person to live with that, never mind to flourish within it. And while it might be obvious that it's hard to be married to a star, what's less obvious is that it is similarly hard to be their brother or sister.

It takes a special kind of person to embrace the challenges of growing up while crammed into a house with our first rivals. As siblings who are raising an aging parent, we must reach for all the humility we can muster as we take inventory of ourselves. We need to look honestly at who we have been as siblings, clean up our acts, and make amends, apologies, admissions, and humble gestures of redemption and reconciliation wherever possible.

As we do that important family work, it's also time to reach out and get out in front of what I call the "sibling pain curve."

Get Proactive

Having examined some of the complexities of sibling relationships, and having taken inventory of ourselves, the next step is to put what we have learned to use by getting out in front of problems. Since we know that the challenges of raising an aging parent are almost guaranteed to bring up sibling conflicts, we can choose to be proactive and open important conversations with our siblings in a constructive and collaborative manner. By doing so, we give ourselves the best possible odds that our family will be able to avoid a few treacherous pitfalls and operate with relative peace as our parents get older.

To that end, here are a few key steps:

- **Become a calm source of information.** Start with good communication. Often, one sibling is more involved in the parent's care than the others, and the effect is that some people feel excluded or simply left out of the

loop. Open the lines of communication, and make sure everyone knows what's happening with Mom's and/or Dad's care. Do so with genuine humility and patience, not with quiet arrogance.
- **Be clear about roles.** This is an area where it's easy to step on one another's toes and create resentment. Some people are attached to doing certain things for Mom and Dad, while others feel they've been doing too much for too long. Now is the time to come to an agreement about who will carry which responsibilities, and decide who, if anybody, is best qualified to serve in that role.
- **Don't undermine.** If your siblings are currently tending to certain aspects of your parents' care, don't undermine those efforts—even if you think they could be doing more, or less, to help your parents. Having a good talk, motivated by your shared love for your parents, and supporting one another's efforts is the best approach. Work with, not against, your siblings.
- **Call out and diffuse rivalries.** This may be the hardest part. It can be very difficult to disentangle old conflicts and rivalries, especially because we sometimes act them out unconsciously. But as you start to notice rivalries coming to the surface, say what you fear is happening. A great deal of change can come from just openly admitting and opting out of jealous dramas. Taking the high road means turning away from destructive passive-aggressive behavior, game-playing, hurtful sarcasm, and jealousies.

- **Finally, do your best to get everyone on the same page.** In order to effectively care for your aging parents, you need everybody to work from the same playbook to the extent that is possible. You want a tempered conversation, focused on what you are we trying to achieve for Mom and/or Dad, and how you are going to go about it, even if that's only achievable with a professional facilitator at the helm.

Of course, these things aren't always possible. I have been called in by hundreds of families for whom just sharing information is a challenge, never mind admitting the way they're feeling or getting everyone to agree to a single plan. Some of us have been going our own ways for too long, and at this point, we aren't motivated to make nice and cooperate with family members. In other cases, siblings simply aren't willing to talk about painful issues from the past.

We may never get the cooperation we're seeking, but by coordinating as many of these elements as we can—goals, clear roles, humble admissions, a game plan—and by limiting rivalrous behaviors, we get out in front of the pain curve and focus our efforts on the opportunity curve. We minimize the possibilities that things will go sideways and spiral out of control with our siblings, and maximize the opportunities that come with working together.

When a Parent Dies

Dormant sibling rivalries can come to the surface when a parent dies. The rawness of making decisions in their final months, weeks, and days of life, as well as planning a memorial service, giving their eulogy, and sorting out myriad issues (including the estate plan) might unleash the very best or worst in us as families. We may find ourselves arguing with doctors and nurses about our parent's medical care, fighting with our brothers and sisters about what to do with Mom's or Dad's stuff, and jockeying to reposition ourselves in the family.

Spewing repressed anger with reckless abandon can divide and potentially irreparably damage sibling relationships. Working together to honor our parents, coming together and letting go of petty differences and grudges, forgiving one another, sharing the workload, and dividing assets equitably will allow us to remain strong as a family.

In a perfect world, we would have sorted out all of these matters with our family members well in advance of the death of our parents, leaving a clear path for everyone to grieve and begin to move forward as a family. The workbook I recommend for covering all these matters in a sensitive and thorough manner was written by my friend, Rosemary Pahl; it is called *Departing Details* (https://www.estateworkbook.com).

The Wisdom to Know What We Can and Cannot Change

Our brothers and sisters were important to how we developed from our first years on this earth, and they continue to be important as we move through this challenging phase of raising, and eventually losing, an aging parent. Whether or not we are successful at bringing a measure of cooperation and peace to our sibling relationships, facing the lifelong issues of sibling rivalry and conflict presents another fertile opportunity for us to ripen and grow as human beings. It calls to mind the wisdom of the Serenity Prayer: "God, grant me the serenity to accept the things I cannot change, the courage to change the things I can, and the wisdom to know the difference."

There will always be things that we just cannot change. We cannot redo our own lives or our siblings' lives. We cannot simply wave a magic wand and change family dynamics or alter people's personalities. But we can choose to approach our brothers and sisters with patience, understanding, humility, fairness, and love. We can do everything in our power to forge a peace between ourselves and our siblings and to be at peace knowing we did our best.

To help you and your siblings talk openly about your aging parents and strengthen your relationship with one another, please go to my website, www.kendruck.com for some very specific coaching tips.

Chapter 7

Rising to the Occasion: The Sandwich Generation

Sometimes adult children spread themselves dangerously thin. Richard, a fifty-four-year-old client of mine, had been the prototypical "good son" to his aging parents, helping them in every possible way. He had also been a loving husband and father to his four kids while running a $20 million company. Then things took a radical turn last year, when his mother fell seriously ill.

Richard's dad, who depended heavily on his wife and with whom Richard never had a particularly close relationship, began to require daily care. This took an overwhelming amount of Richard's time and energy. But that was only half of the problem. Thanks to the new tariffs our government had imposed on his clients in China, he and his team had been putting in ten- to twelve-hour days retooling Richard's business.

Richard's stress level inched higher and higher, little by little, until one morning, while he was driving his kids to school

Raising an Aging Parent

on a day he was supposed to be interviewing a new caregiver and then hosting a business meeting, a car cut in front of him. Right there and then, in front of his kids, he said a few choice words he had never uttered in their presence.

When his twelve-year-old daughter cried out, "Daddy, that's my coach!" he realized that indeed the other driver was his daughter's field hockey coach. And, as it turned out, the coach had actually had the right of way. Fortunately, the coach did not see it was her star player's father cussing her out.

Richard was ashamed of what he had done, both as a father and community member. Leaving his daughter's school for his parents' house, he realized the combined pressures of his business, his parents, and his own family had taken their toll. Something had to change, and this was his wake-up call.

> Just over one of every eight Americans aged forty to seventy is both raising a child and caring for a parent, in addition to between seven and ten million adults caring for their aging parents from a long distance.

Like so many of us, Richard is a member of the "sandwich generation." The Pew Research Center reports that "just over one of every eight Americans aged forty to seventy is both raising a child and caring for a parent, in addition to between seven and ten million adults caring for their aging parents from a long distance."*

Furthermore, "The number of older

---

* https://en.wikipedia.org/wiki/Sandwich_generation

Rising to the Occasion: The Sandwich Generation

Americans aged sixty-five or older will double by the year 2030, to over seventy million," according to the United States Census Bureau. This is also true for millions of "SanGen" ("Sandwich Generation") caregivers in countries like Australia where combining childcare with caring for older or disabled relatives is commonplace.

Carol Abaya, a nationally recognized expert on the SanGen, aging, and elder/parent-care issues in the US, describes three variations of this so-called sandwich generation:

- **Traditional Sandwich**: Those sandwiched between aging parents who need care and/or help and their own children.
- **Club Sandwich**: Those in their forties, fifties, and sixties who are sandwiched between aging parents, adult children and grandchildren—or those in their twenties, thirties, and forties with young children, aging parents, and grandparents.
- **Open-Faced Sandwich**: Anyone else involved in elder care.

In today's SanGen, the kids are the bread on the bottom and the aging parents are the bread on the top. And millions of us are smack in the middle—spread thin and squeezed hard. This has been a reality in my fiancé's and so many of our friend's lives, as well as my own. How we deal with that reality, and whether or not we create a playbook for balancing our lives is another matter.

It's in my nature to plan things out, create strategic plans, and follow a critical path to completion. Whether I am writing another book, helping a client, running a workshop, putting together a new PBS special, or leading a community project. I am continually managing the next undertaking. And while these activities are exciting, they can and do take me away from having any semblance of a personal life. I'm also a fiancé, and a father, and until three years ago, I was the primary caregiver for my ninety-two-year-old mother.

Lucky for me, I've been learning to effectively manage the pressures of being squeezed. When we're feeling pressure from every direction—when we feel as though we're doing heroic things each day just to meet our basic responsibilities—there are a few key strategies that offer precious relief and are eminently worthy of being considered for your SanGen playbook.

You Can Tap the Brakes

Some of our commitments are nonnegotiable: we will continue to be parents as well as sons or daughters, just as we will continue to work and pay the bills. Yet even as some things aren't going to change, it is possible to tap the brakes enough to notice what's happening, to consider what we do have the power to slow down, and to make a few subtle, life and health-affirming changes.

For starters, we may have become so stressed that we haven't been able to step back to see this jam-packed season of life for what it is. Indeed, this may be one of the fullest times of our lives. We have children who need us and parents who need us. A marriage that needs tending. A career or business that needs fostering. And a body that needs care.

Rising to the Occasion: The Sandwich Generation

And while we may feel so stressed that we can barely think, something extraordinary is happening. Our loved ones and our present season of life require our energy and talents, and we are being asked to rise to the occasion as never before—perhaps in a way that will never happen again. It may also be the case that we are so emotionally overwhelmed that we've begun to numb out. A client of mine lost his mother after a long illness, but his life was in such a chaos that he hadn't really taken the time to experience the loss. Then, it hit him like a storm.

Sometimes we are brought to our knees by life. As I experienced quite viscerally after I lost my daughter, there are moments when we are devastated and unable to move. And in those moments of choiceless sorrow, we've hit a new and unfamiliar bottom point. Our life as we knew it is over. We're utterly overwhelmed.

After my daughter's death, I was in despair, and there was no amount of spiritual, religious, or psychospiritual spin—or positive thinking—to help me get over it. That old "getting over it" strategy just didn't work any longer. Neither did such past favorites as an end run, a quick fix, a spiritual bypass, or a good old "I'm too busy to feel anything." Placing my hand over my own heart, acknowledging that I was defenseless against my own sorrow, and holding a flicker of faith that out of this brokenness something in me might grow more whole and heal was the only way through for me.

I had to trust that I would rise up out of the ashes. And until that time, I had to give myself permission to feel what I felt, which was heartsick and broken. Paradoxically, allowing myself to feel utterly broken was what allowed me to begin healing and feeling a new kind of wholeness. I stopped resisting how I felt and that I now walked with a limp in my heart.

Like someone returning home from a war zone, disfigured by what he or she had gone through, I felt deeply wounded, lost and alone. I would have a choice: to devolve into shame, give up hope, and spend the rest of my life wearing a mask—or summon the courage and faith to make my way through this dark night of the soul in hopes of emerging back into some semblance of light. As I bore down and began my grief journey, feeling a new kind of wholeness just behind my brokenness, I could begin to breathe and write new chapters of life.

Rising up from despair, resolving to live an honorable life in the face of losing my daughter, was occasionally met by the desire to give up. Being in the company of people who were dealing with something similar, I could be honest that I felt like giving up and dying. I wanted to tell another man who was complaining about his daughter's tongue ring that I'd "trade straight up" with him. I could also be honest about feeling hopeful that I might somehow be able to go on. Admitting that, I went for a long lunch with a few close buddies. Driving home, I felt a glimmer of hope.

From this glimmer, something much larger began to grow: a non-profit foundation in my daughter's name, the Jenna Druck Center, and a program called Families Helping Families, providing grief support and education to families like my own. Good and noble things had come from my allowing myself to feel broken. Lost. Empty. Alone. And keeping the faith that I could begin to heal slowly from the inside out.

Today you may feel broken, or you may feel more or less okay. But no matter what condition you may find yourself in at this moment, you are caught between caring for your aging parents and the life you have worked so hard to creat . . . you are being challenged to upgrade what I like to call your "self-care operating system." You've tapped the brakes enough to know that it's within your reach to handle your situation better and smarter.

Get started now on taking positive action on a few of the things that are coming up as you continue to read. Write down a few "action items" and put them into your playbook under the title, "Things I Can Do to Effectively Manage My Life in the Sandwich."

A Self-Care Checklist for the Sandwich Generation

To repeat something very important: the only way to survive the squeeze of SanGen stress is to upgrade your self-care operating system. When we feel exhausted and pulled in a million directions, self-management is the key. SanGen survival requires upping your self-care game. At the end of the day, each of us is our own primary-care physician.

> The only way to survive the squeeze of SanGen stress is to upgrade your self-care operating system.

We are responsible for ourselves. Here is a blueprint for taking exceptionally good care of yourself, which you can tailor to meet your particular needs:

- **Exercise.** Whether this means going to the gym or going for a walk, you must move your body. Every day. This may require getting up earlier in the morning, and it might mean saying "no" to others and doing less for them. In my *Self-Care Handbook*, you can outline your program for taking care of your own needs—especially if you are going to continue taking care of others.

- **Eat right.** You will need healthy fuel to power you through this season of life. Pay attention to which foods give you energy and make your body feel good, and which foods make you feel heavy and lethargic. Put the right fuel in your body.

- **Hydrate.** Drink plenty of water—just plain water—every day. Drink less of all the other stuff, by which I mean alcohol and drinks that have been sweetened with sugar.

- **Avoid taking on stress from others**. Whether at work or at home, it's time to determine who gives you energy and who depletes you. The people around you, including family members and co-workers, may come to you to vent or solve their problems. Or you might be accustomed to being a rescuer, doormat, co-dependent enabler, or somebody's "gofer," yet you are stretched too thin to solve problems for others. Now is the time to put up healthy boundaries, and say "no." To say "yes" to giving yourself a break. And to stay strong when invited to go backward.

- **Maintain a positive outlook to the best of your ability.** I used to know an older gentleman who had Parkinson's disease as well as every other physical ailment you could imagine. I was constantly awestruck when he would tell me that the only real handicap in life is a bad attitude—and that they don't give you a parking placard for that. Check in with yourself: *Am I allowing myself to remember all the good stuff that is happening in my life? And balance out the stress?* Be honest with your answer. Remember that each of us is responsible for him- or herself; no one is responsible for my attitude, perspective and/or ability to refocus on the good things of life but me.

- **Stay engaged with your community.** Do you belong to a supportive community? In your neighborhood and/or in your church, synagogue, or mosque? If there is any other type of community, such as Alcoholics Anonymous or another twelve-step program, or a support or study group that nourishes you and gives you a sense of purpose, take full advantage of it. If you don't, think about finding or starting one to balance out the demands of raising an aging parent and dealing with siblings.

- **Make a plan to have fun.** I know, I know; you barely have enough time to go to the bathroom, so how are you going to squeeze in fun? I understand, yet taking pleasure in the good things of this life is an essential part of taking care of ourselves. You might not be able to afford taking time off for yourself, but you cannot afford not to. Look closely at your calendar, and make time to fit in the people and things that make your heart sing. Do it!

- **Waste not**. This is not a time of life when we can afford to stay up watching addictive television programs. Successfully raising an aging parent does not mean worrying about all the things on your to-do list, or having to get up at three in the morning to write one. Landing in a state of sleep deprivation may be a common side effect of SanGen hypervigilance, but it is going to result in "aging parent burnout." Turn the lights out early so that you can rise tomorrow with enough energy to do the things that really matter. And if you need help, find a local sleep clinic and find out how you can begin to get the rest and replenishment you need.

A self-care checklist can be more powerful than it might look at first glance. At its core, taking good care of ourselves is about balancing rest and activity, getting in game shape to play at our life, restoring and rejuvenating our souls, and investing wisely in our best possible futures.

For perhaps as long as we can remember, we may have been running around doing everything for everyone else, leaving ourselves with crumbs and leftovers. It's time for a change.

Rising to the Occasion: The Sandwich Generation

A Few Key Changes Can Make a World of Difference
Richard, the client I described at the beginning of this chapter, eventually told me how he had cursed at his daughter's coach. I recommended a meditation app called Headspace. He took my advice and used Headspace for seventy consecutive days. We also worked on mindfully tightening up his schedule. He knew that he couldn't squander even a moment of any given day, so he became very strategic.

He knew that he'd have to work eleven hours daily or his business wasn't going to make it. He also knew he needed seven hours of sleep each night—not a minute less. Spending two hours a day with his family and one hour at the gym still left enough time for a couple of other things. He attended his twelve-step group at least twice a week, and he made occasional visits to a beautiful park in his town for some treasured leisure time.

Recently, I asked him a question that got us both thinking. If, God forbid, his life ended tomorrow, would there be any part of him crying out, "What about me?" or "Why didn't I take more time?"

He said there are a few creative projects that he's dreamed about but hasn't had the time to begin. He pledged to keep those things on the radar and to start building them into his life just as soon as possible.

In my own darkest and most frantic days, it sometimes took all the strength I had to get myself up and go for a walk. At other times, I could muster the energy to get out on the ocean in my kayak—and out there I found peace in allowing myself permission to just let go. Though it took time and energy to load my kayak and get myself out on the water, this time in nature gave me strength and sustenance.

I wish the same for all of you, my faithful readers. May you find the resolve to get out there—for a walk, a swim, a yoga class, or a bike ride—and may it give you the energy, clarity, perspective, and sense of purpose you need to create more balance in your life, prioritize what's really important, fill your cup, and find peace in knowing you're doing the best you can.

Chapter 8

How Much Is Enough: The Real Responsibilities of Adult Children

This chapter will tackle some of the most difficult decisions we get to make as both aging parents and the adult children of aging parents. What are the responsibilities of an adult child? How much does a good son or daughter have to sacrifice of his or her own needs? How much is enough? And where do we draw the line when it comes to balancing parent care with self-care?

I'm good friends with a lovely couple in their mid-seventies, and unfortunately the wife just recently broke her hip. They're managing well considering the situation, and they are getting support from their older daughter, who lives only a few small towns away, in California. Their younger daughter, who lives in Denver, is expecting her first child. This will be my friends' first grandchild: something that will bring immeasurable joy into their quiet lives. The tricky part is that this newborn will be a thousand miles away, where their daughter and her husband settled after graduate school and where his parents live.

My friends are struggling to figure out their next steps. On the one hand we have a grandmother-to-be dealing with the slow recovery from a broken hip, and on the other hand, we have a thirty-eight-year-old daughter starting her own family and facing the prospect of raising a child who may never get to know his or her maternal grandparents on more than a superficial level. So, who is supposed to travel where? And when? Does Mom get on an airplane with a hip fracture? Do daughter and son-in-law fly to the West Coast with an infant after he or she is born and things have settled.

Or will someone, most likely the grandparents, choose to relocate? In that case, what about the other daughter, whose life is in California? Would a daily FaceTime call from one household to the other, taking into account the one-hour time difference, be enough? And how might any of these decisions affect the son-in-law's parents, who live in Denver? Only one thing is certain: to these questions, there are no simple answers. Most everyone caring for an aging parent will eventually confront the question of how much reorganizing of our lives is enough to accommodate our aging parents?

In many cases, our parents will face similar questions. How much should they adjust their own lives, including a potential relocation, in order to fit themselves into the lives of their adult children and grandchildren? In this situation, the best that any of us can do is take an honest look at the many variables in play, make a plan, and take it for a test drive to see if/how it actually works. Let's start with identifying some of the variables.

First of All, What Is "Enough?"
In assisting an aging parent, and in most areas of our lives, there is no straightforward definition of enough, because it's a concept that means something different for everyone and in every culture. For that reason, determining how much caretaking of our aging parents is enough might start with looking at how we were raised.

Some of us were the oldest child and grew up with an overriding sense of responsibility. Riddled with guilt and a sense of indebtedness, we were hard-wired to be driven and over-achieve. The nature of such a type A personality is that they are calibrated to always do more. No amount of effort ever feels sufficient. In this way of viewing the world, we can't pause, we can't take a deep breath, and we can't take our foot off the gas pedal. This fear of losing status is also often accompanied by a compulsion to prove oneself or compensate for some perceived shortcoming.

There is also the so-called type E person, an individual who aspires to be everything to everyone else and is calibrated to believe that they can never do enough for others. Often, the type E person feels immense pressure to give their undivided attention to those around them. However, the type E personality also lives with a lot of self-doubt and begins to question if what they've offered is the *right* amount of attention. No matter how much they have given, they feel it is never enough. Racked with a sense of obligatory guilt, the type E personality goes so far as to neglect their own health and emotional needs in an effort to give even more attention to those around them.

Then there's the baby in the family. The extreme expression of this is someone who has been coddled and spoiled with a sense of entitlement and expects to be taken care of in any given situation. The idea of being of service or sacrificing for another person has not been wired into their self-involved brains or behavior, nor may it have been learned in adulthood. Because the baby does not see caregiving for an aging mother or father as their job, or feel any sense of responsibility, they are often MIA at the time of their parents' greatest need, a source of deep disappointment to their parents and in conflict with their siblings.

And all of this is to explain why, in beginning to evaluate how much caregiving is enough, we need to assess whether or not we are capable of setting healthy limits and boundaries. Ask yourself if you are the kind of person who always tries to do too much.

Taking the time to understand what drives you and what you need can be life-saving. Checking in with yourself and asking yourself questions such as: Am I driven by a fear of failure and/or inadequacy? Or is it perhaps in my nature to be hesitant, and therefore to do what I later feel was too little? Or, am I comfortable giving and receiving in my relationships? Do I have a fair, balanced and reasonable sense of reciprocity, and where do I draw the line when giving of myself? Or do I act as though I have a hall pass when it comes to talking the least bit of care of my parents as they get older?

Take inventory of where you stand when it comes to the word "enough." As a professor of mine used to say, if you are the kind of person who pushes too hard, this may be a time to back off. Alternatively, if

> Take inventory of where you stand when it comes to the word "enough."

you're the kind of person who is always pulling back, now might be the moment to push forward a bit more. Yet our own history of and orientation to "what's enough" is just one of the issues we need to consider when asking the difficult question of how much care to offer our aging parents.

What Are Our Parents' Needs, and How Are Those Needs Changing?

Some of our parents are extremely independent. They don't want us doting, managing, monitoring or hovering. In fact, we may feel guilty because we continually think we haven't done . . . enough.

"For goodness' sake, Dad, please let me do something for you," we say. "Isn't there anything you need?"

Then there are parents at the other end of the spectrum, whose needs and demands are insatiable. And without realizing it, we may have shaped ourselves to meet those wide-ranging needs. A never-married cousin of mine who had become her mother's caregiver had a special ring tone for her calls. When that school bell went off, she responded like she had been trained. She was allegiant to a fault. Being "on call" to her mother's every whim, she had given up much of her own life. Any other ring tone and she might not even take the call. But with her mom she was spellbound and hell-bent on trying to please her, meet her every need and win her love.

Whether they are independent or demanding, or somewhere in between, our parents also change with time. And so can their need for care. Dad may have been largely autonomous right up until he suffered a stroke. Or what happens when Mom finally concedes that she can't cook for thirty-five people anymore? Life can change quickly or slowly. The concept of "enough" can also change, and your "enough threshold" will likely be tested. Things might be okay right now and change six months from now. Indeed, we will need to continuously recalibrate our assessment of "enough" as circumstances change.

What Sort of Chemistry Do We Have with Our Parents?

In Chapter 6 we talked about how relationships between parents and siblings come in every shape and size. Maybe your brother has always had a special rapport with your parents, while years ago you moved across the continental United States to get as far away from them as possible. Maybe your sister had a falling out with your soon-to-retire father over his succession plan for the family business. The truth, of course, is that some of us have good chemistry with one or both of our parents, while others of us do not. I've seen families for whom one child's uninspired attempts at offering assistance actually upset the mom or dad more than they helped, and triggered conflict between siblings. If we continually butt heads with our parents regardless of our best efforts, it's worth candidly asking ourselves if there is a palpable tension between us? If this is the case, a role in our parents' care may be complicated and require greater thought and possible professional guidance from someone who specializes in working with families.

Alternatively, we may have good parental chemistry and feel close to a loving mother and/or father who took a special interest in us and what was happening in our lives from an early age. And so we may take a genuine interest in their lives, especially as they get older and need us more. Our substantial involvement in each other's lives and care may leave us feeling that we're good sons and daughters, and that we have indeed done enough.

Culture Plays a Role

In some cultures, as alluded to earlier in this book, taking care of aging parents is part of a code of ethics. You move them into your home and care for them until the end, and doing so is a source of honor, high status, and tradition for all involved. It's also a clear responsibility; there is no doubt about what's expected. Some of us may envy that clarity and sense of honor, if not the considerable responsibility attached to it.

But in cultures where the rules concerning aging parents are less clear, there are often muddy and/or unspoken expectations that are voiced indirectly or passive-aggressively. In many families, there is also a considerable guilt factor. Although comedians have joked about the supposed similarities between, say, Jewish and Catholic mothers as capable of "extracting guilt from inanimate objects," guilt permeates families of any cultural or religious origin. If ours is a family that uses guilt to control behavior, we may believe that we're required to perform countless acts of selfless caregiving long before we feel like we've done anywhere near enough. Using guilt, judgement, sarcasm, and suspicion to make somebody feel bad about themselves, control their behavior, and win their loyalty can be a dangerous practice. In the long run, such behavior only breeds distrust, bitterness, and resentment.

When Geography Is a Hurdle

As we saw earlier, proximity can also be a complicating factor. Maybe your parents are in Indiana where they've always lived, but your employer requires you to live in Portland. If the elements of our lives fall into four "boxes"—work, family, health, and spirituality—there are times when we have to choose which is the top priority. Very often, we choose work. We may not be wholly satisfied living across the country from our children's grandparents, but there is no choice, or so it seems.

If seeing our aging parents requires considerable travel, there are a few strategies we can use to make the most of our visits.

Let's say you're planning a five-day sojourn to the East Coast. Since you only have five precious days, you're going to want to make the most of that time; the best approach, then, is to be proactive. Well before your arrival, communicate with parents and siblings about your "ideal itinerary" for your visit:

- Are there certain goals with respect to your parents' care that you or they want to be sure to accomplish? What are they?

- Are there special activities you or they want to do, or particular ways you know you'll want to spend the time with each other? List them.

The work required for such advance planning is well worth it. All too often people come home from family visits feeling disappointed, yet they're relieved. (There's the old Johnny Carson line: "Thanksgiving is the one day in the year that families get together and thank God that they only have to get together one day in the year.") In many cases, however, family visits can provide lifelong memories, if only we make plans ahead of time and get a little "buy-in" from our family members. The key idea here is that we have more control than we may have previously thought over making the amount and quality of our time together a priority.

Form a bold vision of what you'd like to happen during your next long-distance family visit, and then make it happen!

The Only True Answer to How Much Is Enough

Ultimately, there are no one-size-fits-all solutions to questions of how much time and how much care is right to devote to your aging parents. The answer is different for each of us, yet there *is an answer*.

We've now considered how we personally are calibrated—whether we tend to do too much or we tend to hold back—and we've considered our parents' needs, our chemistry with them, our family's culture, and the challenges of geography. Now it's time for the gut-check question.

What is the best that I can do?

Your answer to this question is the only true guide to what constitutes enough. Give yourself the time and space to really consider this question. Search your heart for the answer. But don't forget to factor in the things that might limit you. And please allow it to be a work in progress.

> Your answer to the question, "What is the best that I can do?" is the only true guide to what constitutes enough.

What constitutes enough today is likely to change a few months down the road, and so you will need to make mid-course corrections. Each time circumstances change, you can come back to this question and reevaluate: "What is the best that I can do right now?"

How Much Is Enough: The Real Responsibilities of Adult Children

If you show up in the moment and do the best you can, you will have the right to be at peace and feel proud of yourself for being a good son or daughter. And if doing your best is, for some reason, still not enough, you need to be clear about what more you might have asked of yourself and whether it is truly reasonable. Unreasonable expectations lead only to needless, senseless feelings of failure and unhappiness.

There Will Be Trade-Offs

In my perfect world, and looking in the proverbial rear-view mirror, I probably could have been a better son. Hindsight might tell me that there were times when I could have been more understanding, forgiving and patient. In a perfect world, I would have been kinder and less critical, with a more loving temperament. But, since we don't live in a perfect world, and since I am not a perfect person, I strive to accept that I did the best I could in loving my father and mother.

Those of us with an overactive inner critic may have to work at this by changing the way we talk to ourselves. Learning to take your foot off of your own throat and place your hands gently on your own hearts may take time and practice. But freeing yourself of this false sense of indebtedness, or perfectionism, can be a liberating, life-changing gift.

We may have had to stay painfully rooted in a city that was a thousand miles from our parents at the end of their lives. We may think back on what we wished we would've said to them. Or, for a variety of reasons, we may have had to pull back some of our efforts when they needed us. Perhaps we wore ourselves out doing everything we could, and as a result, suffered caregiver burn out and collapsed into exhaustion. Or maybe we could never find a way to overcome feelings of anger and resentment, and we still feel guilty because of it.

We are all imperfect people in an imperfect world. Many of the variables that affect how we care, or don't care, for our aging parents are out of our hands. So we try to do the best we can. And, to the best of our abilities, we search our souls to make peace with the fact that there was a limit to what we could give. Realizing now that we could have said or done more, we can do the next best thing and offer it up to our parents posthumously. In my mind, it's never too late to give of our love and gratitude.

We're Doing the Best We Can and So Are They
My dad, who grew up in poverty, never got so much as a hug from his own father. And when he became a father himself, his approach was to be harshly critical of me for reasons that had everything to do with his own Depression-era upbringing. My dad's fiery words, "Use your head, stupid!" resounded in my ears nightly and painfully. And I swallowed his criticisms whole. To protect my fragile sense of self, I did what young kids do when they feel under attack. I tuned people out and looked for opportunities to prove my worth.

Becoming a star athlete provided newfound confidence. But for the first twenty-five years of my life, I struggled in school and questioned whether I was, in fact, "stupid." Trained to protect myself from incoming criticism, I was desperate for positive validation and caught myself looking for it in a few unhealthy ways, such as bragging about and even embellishing my accomplishments.

In time, and as I became interested in psychology, I began to figure things out. I learned that I was actually very smart but not in the ways that most schools measure. After graduating from college and getting married, I discovered what it meant to be a loving, supportive husband and a good father. And I learned how to use my sensitivities in working with people and advocating for social change.

After completing graduate school and getting my doctorate, I created a men's workshop, Alive and Male, and began offering it across the United States. In the workshop, everyone wore a name tag that bore his first name, with his dad's name underneath. And we introduced ourselves in a way that evoked powerful feelings about our fathers.

"I am Ken," I would say, "the son of Charles."

In those workshops the first exercise was to break into small groups and tell the story of what had and had not happened in our relationships with our fathers. The results were incredibly moving and healing in a way I could not have predicted.

Before I started giving that workshop, though, I had taken my dad aside and apologized to him. I told him that I realized I'd always taken Mom's side, acting as her protector and champion. Looking back, I had been judging him unfairly without any real understanding of what was going on in his life. I told him I loved him and was sorry. I forgave him for his harsh criticisms, telling him that I now understood it was his way of trying to teach me how to be a man and to love me. I thanked him profusely for the years of hard work he had put into providing for his family, paying for my education and opening his heart to his family members.

Then I decided it was my responsibility to teach him everything I was learning about being a good and loving man. He'd learned nothing from his own father about men expressing affection for one another. I took on this challenge as something that I could do. Because of that, in the last years of his life, we enjoyed a relationship of deep love.

I have a precious memory of the two of us walking down Fifth Avenue in New York and stopping in front of the window of a B. Dalton bookstore, where my father could see copies of my first book. We walked arm in arm, and I remember his pulling me close. It was as though, toward the last years of his life, he had finally learned how to be a loving, supportive father and grandfather. Something had freed up the love inside of Charles Druck.

It wasn't long afterward that he passed away. In a sense, our relationship had become one of the great blessings of my life. I loved my dad so dearly. And I knew I didn't want to carry the burden of anger and resentment of what could have been or should have been. I wanted to live in the deep gratitude I felt for my father. We are who we are, and our parents are who they are.

What would we say on their death bed to a father or a mother who could not forgive him- or herself, who was apologizing and trying to make amends?

"Mom/Dad, you did the best you could with what you had. Thank you for loving me."

The best testament to the job they did is right in front of them: It's you, their children. And their grandchildren. Your parents weren't perfect, and they didn't do everything right. But what they did was somehow enough, and here you are. As I bond with my grandchildren, I hope that I am able to continue to pass down this message to them, and that they will pass the message along to their children, and so on. It is this message that helps to create a healthy cycle of love and understanding from generation to generation.

To the best of your ability, try to love them with your whole heart. Give them your thanks and your blessing for what life with them has been, for better or worse. Wish them peace and tell them again and again how grateful you are and how much you love them.

Chapter 9

Making the Tough Calls: Where They Live, What They Spend, What Medical Care They May Need

There are certain moments in our lives as parents when our kids come to us with problems that they've been wrestling with on their own.

"Dad, I'm getting bullied in school."

"Mom, I think I'm failing math."

"Dad, I like this boy but he doesn't even know I exist."

"Mom, I want to try out for the soccer team but I'm scared."

As parents, these can be profound moments for us because we see that our child trusts us and is stepping forward to openly share what they're facing. We may find ourselves getting emotional or becoming protective, because we immediately feel their pain.

But these moments may also be a struggle for us because our first impulse is to simply step in and solve the problem for them. And this would clearly not be the best way to help them. If we hear our child is getting bullied in school, our first instinct is probably to run out the door, find that bully, and kick him or her in the rear end. That's not our best recourse though, and it's probably not what our son or daughter wants us to do either.

"Daddy, please don't do anything crazy," your daughter might say, taking a step back. She is in distress and wants your help, but she doesn't want you to overreact by swooping in and rescuing her.

In a number of ways, this can be similar to what we do with our aging parents when we learn of their distress. Our first impulse is to step in and solve the problem for them, sorting through their options and determining the best strategy for alleviating their pain. Instead, the best place to start is simply to acknowledge them for trusting us enough to share their problems. And the very first thing to do after that is to say, "Thank you."

Listen & then Ask What They Are Thinking

The next step is to listen and find out what's weighing heavily on our parent's mind or heart. Maybe they saw something on television that scared them. Perhaps they have been thinking about doing a reverse mortgage. The moment an aging parent mentions the words "reverse" and "mortgage" in the same sentence, we become worried. Enrolled as our parent's security guard and protector, and fearing how vulnerable they are to vultures who groom and prey upon the elderly, we may launch into a lecture on all the problems and pitfalls of all the financial schemes being shopped to seniors on TV these days.

Instead of allowing ourselves to get carried away by our own first reaction, we can direct our focus to where our parent is in their own thinking. To find out, we can pose some open-ended questions. "I'd be glad to talk to you about this, Mom," we can say. "Tell me, what have you been thinking about getting a reverse mortgage?"

Where an aging parent should live—in the home they've always had, in a downsized condo or apartment, or in a retirement or assisted-living community—is one of the most difficult logistical issues they, and we, will likely face as they get older. A parent who has been residing in the family home for half a century may privately start to wonder if it's the best place for them. This could be the result of mounting financial pressure or spurred on by the fact that they just don't have the energy to maintain a large household anymore. Maybe their brother or sister has moved into a retirement community and loves it there. Or perhaps all of their old neighbors have either moved out of the old neighborhood or passed away and they are beginning to feel out of place.

When a parent raises a question about their living situation, it can take time for them to reveal their actual underlying concerns that may be underlying the question. When you first ask them to share what they're thinking, ten minutes of highly emotional discussion might be enough for them to start. Check in to see if they want to launch into a full-blown conversation by asking if this a good time for all of you to discuss their options. And if they become overwhelmed or confused, it may be the right time to stop.

By allowing them to steer the conversation, and respecting their wishes, you may be surprised by what they ultimately share. Maybe your parents are thinking about downsizing and that spurs a conversation about financial planning.

A Courageous Aging audience member once told me, "Ken, folks are living longer, and it's not uncommon for people my age to outlive their savings." He explained, "With the cost of health care, older parents like me run into financial trouble and need to turn to their kids for help."

An aging parent who is questioning whether or not to stay in the family home, may not initially open up about their financial troubles, especially if you launch into your own long-winded response. By inviting them to share whatever they're thinking, and to do so on their own timeline, they are likely to be more forthcoming about the fears they're really facing.

When it comes to making the tough calls in this phase of life, only one thing is certain: it will be emotional and require a great deal of patience and understanding on your part.

Sorting Through Options While Honoring Family Bonds

There are things we can learn as we watch our aging parents either avoid or take care of their affairs. Getting good life insurance and health care may be two of them. Staying fit, mentally and physically, may be another. And paring down one's stuff is a goal we should all take note of.

In the past couple of years, I've started decluttering my home and office. I know that if I don't do it, the task will eventually fall to my daughter, fiancé, nephew, sister, brother or other family member. For that reason, I have started sorting through everything that's accumulated under my roof. At times this has been extremely challenging!

We're not just talking only about the sorting through the possessions of Ken Druck, including forty-five years of professional files, scrapbooks, memorabilia and artwork; I also have precious things that tell the story of my earth and angel daughters' lives, carefully stored in a shed full of plastic bins, each with its own label. And my mother's belongings, including things from her parents that originated in the Jewish shtetls of Europe, have also been saved. There are wood-framed pictures of my great grandparents, silver kiddush cups and boxes of other priceless mementos. And this doesn't even include her furniture, beautiful antique pieces that I'd been holding onto until my daughter and her husband had them refinished and found a new home for them in the beautifully decorated baby room of their twins.

Now, as I begin my own decluttering, I'm trying to pass these heirlooms on to the next generation, only to discover that my daughter and my nephews don't want most of these things! They say it's too much; the furniture's "too big" and "doesn't fit in our house." Of course, that presents a dilemma for me. What should I do with the things that represent our collective family history? How am I going to lighten my load and unclutter my home and office so the people I love do not inherit a huge mess?

I mention this experience because the hardest transitions for our parents are often difficult precisely because of the emotional terrain underneath. What to do with my mother's dresser isn't really about a piece of furniture. It's about family history and memory, my daughter's bond with her Bubby, and my grandchildren having something that was once cherished by their great-grandmother. And the same is true when it comes to our parents' decision to stay, or not, in their longtime home.

Before we go further into how we make the toughest decisions, now is a good time to think about how you and your family might want to preserve your collective history. A big oak dresser might be impossible to keep, but digital files take up no room at all. Should I capture some of our precious things on a digital camera and give the rest of my things away to people who can make good use of them? Might it also be a good time to pull out a voice recorder and ask Mom to tell her story? Here is where technology can be a blessing to your family.

I was surprised by what happened when I started really listening to tales of my family history that I had heard only in passing. I'd always known that my uncle had the best stories about my father, things that my father himself would never tell me. Meanwhile, for my entire life I'd wondered why my Dad always insisted on spending such a long time in the shower.

Making the Tough Calls

When I was a child, I would stand outside the bathroom door knocking gently and calling, "Hey, Dad, are you okay in there?"

It wasn't until I started recording our family history on tape that I learned from my father's older brother, my Uncle Steve, the reason behind Dad's interminable showers. He was the youngest of five and grew up in utter poverty in the Bronx. Once a week the family would carry a warm pot of water up five flights of stairs and dump it into the bathtub. My father was the youngest, so he was the last in that tub. He got to bathe once a week in his brothers' used bathwater.

Forty years later, he was still washing off the dirt. My whole life I'd judged my father. But hearing this story, I found myself wondering how I could judge this man when I'd never understood his history.

Most of the time we don't know the history and the feelings that drive our parents and our grandparents to act and feel the way they do. They may not be consciously aware of these things either. Even without our knowing the specifics, though, it's likely that if they're facing a major life transition, they're wrestling with some deep emotions related to something in their personal history.

It's deeply human to want to save that history. By creating an opportunity for our parents to share and record their stories, and the stories of their parents, we may give them a great sense of relief and peace, belonging to both the known history and the unknowable mystery that is hidden within this vast universe and great expanse of time. We are also giving ourselves, and our children, an enormous gift—the gift of knowing where we came from, our family history and what happened that shaped our lives. Although we may not fully appreciate this until much later in life, it is a heritage that can be passed on with great benefit to future generations with great benefits. And today, doing so can be as simple as taking out a smartphone and turning on the video camera or recording a voice memo. With the recorder rolling, we can sit beside them and hold their hand. We are right there with them as they tell their stories of how they made their life their own. This is a way of remembering, savoring, cherishing and appreciating the life they have lived and saying a grateful goodbye to things they've lost. By accompanying them through this process and encouraging them to tell their stories, we give them permission to bless their life and to make peace with their past.

Stepping Toward Agreement

Whether or not our parents choose to discuss the twists and turns in their lives with us depends on many things. All we can do is make it safe for them to open up and confide in us. They may ultimately prefer to keep their stories to themselves or to share them with another confidante. We might not like that, but that's the way it is. They may also stubbornly refuse to tell us anything about how they feel or what they want, or deal with difficult decisions altogether.

"I don't want to talk about it," they may say, "Let's talk about that some other time.

"Stop nagging me. I'll figure it out myself."

If we see them resisting what we believe is a necessary transition, or putting themselves at risk, we might have a few backup plans ready to go. As I have said, taking a more active role with an aging parent and changing the playbook can be difficult. You will need to take it one step at a time.

> Whether or not our parents choose to discuss the twists and turns in their lives with us depends on many things. All we can do is make it safe for them to open up and confide in us.

One prudent way to move forward is to ask your parents to take a small exploratory step. "Dad, will you please just go with me to visit a retirement community I like," you might ask, "Let's just see what the options are, and then we can talk about it later."

Or maybe the dilemma isn't about where they live. Maybe it's something to do with their health. We can ask them to take one small step forward on this front, too. "Mom, will you agree to let me make a doctor's appointment for you?" you can ask. "And let me come with you?"

In one family I worked with, the aging mother was showing signs of depression. Over time her kids came to believe she was quite depressed, although she would never admit as much. One of her kids suggested the possibility of her trying a mild antidepressant—only to be met with an adamant "No." Her mom didn't think it was appropriate to talk openly about her mental health or take medicine for it.

But she trusted her doctor, and she wasn't opposed to having one of her kids accompany her to an appointment. There, in a confidential setting with a trusted third party, Mom's stance softened.

"That could be great for you," the doctor said when they broached the possibility of an antidepressant. Ultimately, Mom went for it. But if her kids alone had done the lobbying without help from a trusted outsider, she wouldn't have budged. A month later, it was clear to everybody, including the mother, her adult children and the staff of the retirement community, that her taking a mood-elevating antidepressant had been a life-changing decision.

This is an approach that can also work with money matters.

"Dad, will you please come with me to talk to an expert on how best to handle family finances? Talking with them about what your options are might be very helpful."

Sometimes the experience and advice of an expert shifts something inside us. We see the situation differently or open up to new possibilities we would not have considered.

Drawing on what we covered earlier, another useful approach is to make sure all siblings are on the same page. If a parent is resisting a needed transition, or getting much-needed help, it's best if the kids are aligned as they present a single suggestion or request.

Indeed, with all siblings in agreement, it's possible to orchestrate a gentle conversation or, if needed, a soft intervention—nothing fancy, nothing that will feel to our parents like they're being put on the spot, cornered or pressured into doing something. But if you are all standing around the kitchen counter munching on mixed nuts, it might be a good moment to say, "Dad, please give this a try. All of us feel like it would be a good thing for you. And for us. Please trust us on this, Dad."

Whose Decision Is It Anyway?

When our children are young and come to us with a dilemma, our job is to help them think through their options and perhaps narrow them down to the best ones. Then it's up to them to decide—unless, of course, we are still their legal guardians and we see them acting irresponsibly. Before our kids turn eighteen, we have the authority to make decisions for them, and we're likely to use that authority if we see them making poor decisions.

But when it comes to an aging parent, we have no such authority. Even if we have come to believe our parents aren't capable of making sound decisions, there's a difference between our judgment of their competence and whether or not they're viewed as competent in the eyes of the law.

The law of the land does not authorize us to automatically become legal guardians to our aging parents when they turn, say, eighty-five. They may experience cognitive decline, start getting into car accidents, refuse to see a doctor when they need one, or mindlessly do business with a bogus vendor.

We may make compelling arguments for them to take responsibility and call upon the criminal justice system to help protect them, but we do not have the legal authority to make decisions on their behalf.

Okay, It's Their Decision. What Now?
There may come a time when something a parent is doing, or not doing, is endangering them or someone else, and that is the point at which the adult child makes an executive decision. For example, since we may not have the power to put the family home up for sale, our only option may be to intensify our own involvement in the situation.

"Dad, it no longer works for you to live in this house. I know this is your home and you love it here, but we need to find you a better living situation. I'm no longer willing to do all the things that make it possible for you to stay here, but I am willing to help you find a new place. Talk to me!"

We do this only after we have tried everything else. This is our last resort.

They May Resist, and They May Retaliate
In one family I worked with, an aging uncle had deteriorated to the point that he was a danger to himself as well as to others. On more than one occasion, he left the stove on and almost burned his house down. He and his wife, and all of the people who lived in his apartment complex could have died. By that point, of course, it was imperative that he relocate to

an elder-care facility and receive custodial care. And yet he still refused to cooperate. Eventually his family had no choice but to move him against his will.

Was it ugly? Yes.

Was it sad? Terribly.

Was it necessary? Again, yes.

In some cases, the aging family member will use any power they have to retaliate against the kids or relatives who have, in their eyes, "betrayed" them. This may come in the form of a threat, such as "Back off or I'm cutting you out of my will." Or it may take the form of a punishment. Rather than using an economic weapon like an inheritance, or retracting support, some parents start badmouthing an offending child to the rest of the family, or excluding them from family gatherings.

"I'm worried about your sister; she's been acting like a lost soul," they say, trying to pull the other siblings over to their side. In this way the child who is most willing to speak out against a parent's misbehavior becomes the proverbial messenger who gets shot, and the perpetrator of a crime.

"Your sister has made your mother and me miserable," they might say in such a situation. "Your brother is destroying our family." "You've got to do something about your brother and sister. Please."

Part of this tactic, called deflection, is producing evidence to show that the entire problem was caused by the child. This is deeply manipulative and usually taps into old, toxic blame patterns from within the family structure. The story I shared earlier about a father who owned a family business and badmouthed his son to his siblings and colleagues was an example of turning an adult child who speaks up into the one with the problem. Sadly, it is not uncommon for retaliatory parents to turn a disfavored child of any age into the family symptom carrier by questioning their character.

Not long ago I was at a friend's birthday party. While we were all sitting around a long table, an elderly woman started talking about estate planning. This sparked a whole conversation, and everyone started sharing things they were hoping to do for their kids or grandkids. A grandmother at the table admitted she had saved up throughout her entire life for her children and grandchildren, and that she felt guilty about spending a few thousand dollars on a Caribbean cruise. Then one woman, who was visiting from out of town and had been quiet throughout the discussion, spoke up.

"You know what I'm going to do?" she said. "I'm going to spend every penny! My kids are getting nothing!" No one knew what to say in response. It was clear that she'd been through a painful experience with her kids and was hell-bent on punishing them by leaving a legacy of vindictiveness.

Mired in pain and resentment, some parents will just let a family problem fester. They may never bring it up directly. It may only come out in little passive-aggressive jabs, subtle threats, or sarcastic comments. Adult children don't discover they have been written out of a parent's will until that parent passes away, and by then, of course, it's too late to do anything about it.

For all of these reasons, it is important to approach toxic family systems with great sensitivity and care. In the case of the father who owned the family business, it took six months of hard work in coaching to unravel the conflicts and resentments that were buried, sort things out, and begin the healing process.

We Do Our Best to Leave a Legacy of Love

As we'll explore in the final chapters of this book, the most important thing we can do in raising an aging parent is to be loving in all the ways we can. We aren't perfect, and neither are they. We won't always be at our best. But if we screw things up and cause each other pain, we can take action to restore good faith and trust by assuring each other of our love.

"I'm sorry, Mom. I love you and didn't mean to hurt you."

"Dad, I made this decision because I love you and am concerned about your safety and well-being."

No matter how hurt by, angry with, or estranged from our parents (or our adult children) we may be, we must also remind ourselves that life is short. In most cases, we can say and do a multitude of things to restore love and trust and get things back on track. This includes apologizing, showing an inordinate amount of compassion, acknowledging how hard this is, and being demonstrably affectionate and grateful. o A sincere, "Papa, I'll never forget the way you were there for me, and I love you so much," or a father saying back to his son,

"I'll never forget the way you were there for me and I love you so much," is often enough to close a chasm between an adult child and his or her aging parent. If your father, mother, or your child has died or is estranged, you can tap into the love that never dies to find forgiveness.

Chapter 10

Living Losses: Diminishment, Dementia, Dishonor

A year after I founded the Jenna Druck Center and launched the Families Helping Families program, something completely unexpected happened. We started getting phone calls from parents whose children were still alive, but these parents were grieving nonetheless. These parents had children who were struggling with addiction, debilitated by an accident, or incapacitated by a mental or physical illness such as cancer. Or they were separated from their children, either because a child was estranged, incarcerated, deployed, missing, or lost to them in some other way.

The future that these parents had envisioned for their children and their families was either lost forever or, at least, in great peril. These parents felt helpless and were living under a dark cloud of fear. As I got to know many of them, I realized they were suffering from something I came to call "living losses." Their loved one was still alive, and yet was very much lost to them. The future they envisioned had been obliterated. As a result, just like bereaved families who have suffered a life loss, these families were heartbroken and in dire need of understanding, emotional support, and guidance, as well as resources to help their children and themselves.

Our society has yet to recognize the severity of pain and trauma associated with such living losses or to provide adequate resources to those who are suffering from them. The Jenna Druck Center began inviting these families to come together to support one another, develop effective intervention and survival strategies, and to share vital information with one another. The Living Losses Support Group, 50 percent of whom were parents of alcoholics and addicts, became a pillar of our work at the center.

But for most people suffering from living losses, this type of grief goes unrecognized. In this chapter we'll explore the living losses we grieve as our parents age, and the impact they have on us. We'll look at what we can do to help ourselves and our parents deal with these unwelcome changes, and learn how to manage the ones that are beyond our control.

Diminishment: From Forgotten Words to Changed Personality—Losing the Father I Knew

Diminishment can be so subtle that it sneaks up on us. Maybe we're having a visit with our parent and they can't remember the name of someone important—this, from the parent who had always remembered everyone they'd ever met. Maybe the forgetful parent just told you the story last week. Or perhaps such a parent struggles to find the right words, and this struggle has become the rule rather than the exception. Throughout your entire life, you've admired your parent's sharp mind, and now it's changing right before your very eyes.

Or perhaps it's your parent's physical abilities that are in decline. The dad who used to be a tower of strength is too weak to climb the stairs. The mom who used to lead the way on hikes now watches from the car as she fights valiantly to heal from knee surgery. With doctors' appointments, medications, and health concerns on the rise, we may be seeing our parent as vulnerable and even frail for the first time in our life.

Changes in their personality can also leave us feeling as though we're slowly losing them. Perhaps they were always the type who loved life and relished being around other people, and now that is changing. They're becoming cynical, bitter, short-tempered and even rude. The time they used to spend conversing with friends or reading is now spent alone staring out the window or watching television.

The source of personality change may not be a mystery: many people become depressed as they get older because they feel lonely or isolated. Perhaps their spouse of fifty years, closest sibling, or best friend has passed away, and they're trying to go on with their own life while grieving that loss and carrying that pain. They may no longer have the sense of identity they had previously, whether their occupation was raising kids or running a business. They now have no occupation, routine, or schedule at all. They don't have the same social circle they've always had, and their adult children and grandkids often seem to be "too busy" for a visit. They may feel overwhelmed by technology, the relentless stream of breaking news on television, and fears about unbridled artificial intelligence as the world around them changes. Or they may feel overlooked—even invisible—in group situations, as nobody asks their opinion about anything anymore. Amid all these changes, they may also lose their faith. They may not know what they believe at this point in their life, and that can make them doubly cynical and despairing in the way they view the world.

A lifelong Democrat, my mother used to switch back and forth between CNN and MSNBC. One day, she called me in tears after having mistakenly watched the news on Fox. "Ken, our world is broken," she said, "and I don't know if or how we're going to fix it." At age ninety-two, having seen the world turn through seven United States presidents, she was in absolute despair about the current one.

My dad, on the other hand, had always been a really ornery type of guy—until he found himself very sick with heart failure. On occasions when he was in the hospital, afraid that he was about to die, he would soften, becoming more loving and approachable. Indeed, in addition to living losses, there are also living gains. Our parents may become the more loving and generous versions of themselves in this phase of life, and that can be a real boon. We always knew my dad was feeling better when he went back to his usual ornery self, which was a mixed blessing.

When we see our parents lose their mental or physical faculties and become diminished, we feel a sense of loss. Whether we admit it or not, something important is changing. The mother or father we have now is no longer the mother or father we always knew. The parents who were the foundation of our lives are still here with us—and yet, whether we know it or not, they are no longer the same people we knew and loved. And, of course, we have our own lives and families to take care of. This situation represents a living loss like no other. When we essentially lose a parent who is still living, a dark sadness creeps over us.

Dementia: The Loss of Understanding— and Connection

Recently, as I watched my daughter and her husband prepare for parenthood, I began getting myself ready to be a grandpa. This period has been a joy-inducing highlight of my life.

Significant advances in our knowledge, skills, and best practices for raising a child have revolutionized prenatal and infant care, cognitive development, nutrition, and education in almost every area of children's health and wellbeing. All of these advancements in science are also relevant to raising an aging parent, because we understand more than ever before about preventing cognitive, physical, and psychosocial decline. We may encourage our parents to take silver-age yoga classes, share with them exciting new research on preventing cognitive decline and Alzheimer's disease, or gift them our parents with geriatric nutrition coaching. Upgrading our knowledge, skills, and best practices for raising an aging parent helps to make us better sons and daughters.

Even as we do the very best we can, however, dementia is something that many of our families will still need to face.

Several chapters ago, I wrote about one of the most powerful experiences we as human beings can have: looking into the eyes of another person and feeling truly understood. It's an experience that strikes us in our core, and frequently leads to a deepening in our relationship with that person. When we are in the presence of someone suffering from dementia, some part—or perhaps most—of that person is gone. We experience their physical body and we may catch glimpses of the person they always were, but they are not here with us in the old way. Now, when we look in the parent's eyes, searching for glimpses of the person we knew and loved, that person we knew is not there. The pathway for affection, empathy, and compassion—which used to flow back and forth—has been lost. Dementia brings with it all of the challenges and sorrow that accompany diminishment, and it goes further: when our loved ones suffer from dementia, we look into their eyes as we have a thousand times before, but the understanding, affection, and history of all we have been through is gone. This brings on unspeakable grief, yet another type of devastating living loss.

Grappling with grief in my own life and watching my mother get older, I have turned again and again to what Barbara Kingsolver wrote in the book *Animal Dreams*. "You don't think you'll live past it. And you don't, really," she said. "The person you were is gone. But the half of you that's still alive wakes up one day and takes over again."

The parent we knew is gone. This changes *us* too. In the face of such loss, we aren't the same person we used to be either. But there's a half of us that's still here, and in time that half will summon the courage and strength to suffer this loss, figure out how to go on, and even begin writing new chapters of life. This is the path of honor.

Taking the Path of Honor: How Good Choices Lift an Entire Family

In the last chapter we covered some of the toughest choices we, and our parents, must make as we move through this challenging phase of life. At the end of the chapter we discussed the prospect of extremely difficult parents who resist and try to retaliate against or reject family members who don't agree with their choices.

If our parents continue to make poor choices despite our most loving attempts to intervene, there is another consequence that is likely to result: chaos. Our parents may engage in activities—perhaps in the realms of finances, medications, or behaviors that endangers others—that lead them (and us) to chaos, disorder, and humiliation. Despite our wishes and our best attempts to dissuade them, they act in a bad way. Excruciating consequences follow, and we, as their son or daughter—and indeed our entire family—find ourselves in a state of chaos. Faced with this situation through no fault of our own, what choice do we have? How can we move forward?

I once worked with someone whose father was put in jail for unlawful financial dealings. My client wasn't surprised that the situation had sunk to this level. It wasn't the first time he'd been called to rescue his dad in some way or another. This time, though, he chose not to bail his father out. The offending behavior had become a destructive pattern, and rescuing Dad only would have enabled him to continue as before. For my client and his family, tough love was the only way forward.

When we face chaos as a result of our parent's actions, we may be out of our minds with anger and embarrassment. We may say to ourselves over and over, *"I can't take it anymore."* Whether we distance ourselves from them because we have run out of patience, or whether we seek counsel from a family therapist, or even take a faith-based approach and turn to God, is an important decision requiring careful deliberation.

Start this deliberation by finding a safe place to reflect. Before you fall into an old pattern of intervening or rescuing, or before you say something you'll regret, it's a good idea to vent. The situation is awful, and it's been causing you stress, perhaps for years. Now is the time to let off some steam. And as you do so, you may find yourself saying, "I'm done! I don't want any part of this. I won't have anything to do with them. Give me a parentectomy!" It's important to let yourself feel this sooner rather than later.

Now that you have vented and cleared the air a bit, you can move toward taking inventory. "What are my options?" you can ask yourself. "And what am I willing to put up with? And not put up with? Can I resign myself to living in a world of second and third or even more chances? Do I have it in me to give my parents yet another chance? If so, what terms and conditions do I have for getting involved? What would it look like if my parent does what I'm asking? What will the consequences be if my parent gets with the program? And what will the consequences be if that doesn't happen? Is there anybody or anything else that might stand in the way of executing this plan? If so, how can I deal with that now?"

As with my client who decided not to bailout his father, it's important to notice whether or not your behavior has served to enable theirs. My client had always rescued his father. It took him years, if not decades, to realize that by doing so, he had become part of the problem. No longer reinforcing his father's behavior, he became part of the solution.

As you evaluate how to proceed from here, it's important to put an end to any habits of enabling. It's likely that this move will be met with still more vitriol from your parent. My client's father was angry and astonished when his son wouldn't bail him out, especially because it was easily within the son's financial means to do so. He didn't let his father's cries of abandonment sway him. He was done being his father's enabler and perpetuating the problem.

My client had to distance himself from his father for a lengthy time. They had almost no contact during that period. Sometimes my client felt overwhelmed by guilt and doubt. *Am I doing the right thing?* he wondered. *Am I being a good son?* He wasn't certain that he was handling the situation the best way possible, but he was certain that he could no longer put up with an old pattern that was also hurting his father.

There came a time when the father expressed deep remorse for what he had done and for the pain he'd inflicted on his family. He began to earn back his son's trust, little by little. Eventually, his son helped him back on his financial feet.

Not every story has such a happy ending of a parent's redemption. Sometimes we have to draw a line in the sand and take charge of our parents if/when they are not willing and/or capable of making good decisions. This is one of those "easier said than done" things to do. It can be very difficult. We must step back and reassure ourselves that we've done the right thing, and that tough love is still love, which may take time, faith, and raw courage.

The Real Grief of Living Losses

Whether we're grappling with our aging parent's diminishment, dementia, or need for tough love, the emotional

Living Losses: Diminishment, Dementia, Dishonor

reaction within us is going to be some variety of grief. In one way or another, we are losing the parent we always knew, and that triggers a deep sorrow within us.

We may not acknowledge that we're grieving: in fact, many of us don't. Often without realizing it, we may begin avoiding or denying our feelings, perhaps even self-medicating to numb the sadness. Once again, we have a choice. We can deny and avoid, or we can allow ourselves to feel, to begin processing our emotions. And when we allow ourselves to experience what we're feeling, we set in motion something akin to healing from a physical injury.

> Whether we're grappling with our aging parent's diminishment, dementia, or need for tough love, in one way or another, we are losing the parent we always knew, and that triggers a deep sorrow within us.

Think about how incredible our bodies are. We perform miracles with every breath. Our blood brings oxygen and other nourishment to our organs, muscles, and other tissues, washing away toxins and replenishing life. We are unconsciously in a constant state of repair and regeneration. And when we suffer a physical injury, our bodies know just what to do. Through the miraculous systems in place within each of us, our bodies commence healing.

Our emotional system works in much the same way. When we grieve, our system gets a kind of internal signal that says, "I'm feeling sad. I'm feeling scared." From that point, we can organically begin to process the emotional injury and heal. But when we don't allow ourselves to process the emotions, we arrest the healing process. Often what we do instead is, we shoot the messenger. We decide we can't deal with feeling sad or scared, so we push it away or turn it into something else.

But we can choose to allow ourselves to grieve. Let me say that again: *we can choose to allow ourselves to grieve.* We can decide to experience this sense of loss that's already present. We can give ourselves permission to be human and proceed with honesty and integrity, even though it's a sad truth we are allowing.

As part of our grieving, we can also let ourselves voice our "objection" to the universe. Allowing ourselves to yell or wail at the forces we know are bigger than us opens up a world of healing. "I hate this!" we may say. "It's not fair that my mother has Alzheimer's! Don't ask me to just sit here and accept this abomination of nature. Get me someone in customer service! Now!"

Shortly after my daughter's death, I had a life-changing experience. I had been railing at God, "How could YOU let this happen?" God was, after all, supposed to watch over everything, including my daughter on that bus headed toward the Taj Mahal. After several hours of tearful anger, I had nothing left.

"Let's have your child die and see how YOU feel," I yelled with a vengeance, picturing God right in front of me. And then, in an instant, everything changed. In a moment of revelation, I saw a tear in the eye of God. God was crying with me. This was not God the puppeteer, who watched over everything and had allowed my daughter to die in a violent bus crash. It was an eminently compassionate God who was the force of good and love in the world.

From that point on, I felt that God was with me, that I was not alone, that my suffering was being held in a mysteriously divine expression of compassion. By allowing myself those hours of rageful grief, giving myself permission to cry out and spit in the face of the universe, and voicing my objection to what had happened, I was able to begin to understand life's real terms, to reconcile with the fact that life is not fair, to commence a long healing process, and to feel the presence of a higher power.

I still don't fully understand what happened that day. Yet I know that the measure of comfort I found was possible only because I had allowed myself to object, and to grieve fully without holding back.

The Power in Finding Compassion for Ourselves

As we grapple with living losses, we help ourselves by allowing the grieving process to run its natural course. Our pain and sense of loss is real and often choiceless. Shifting the way we talk to ourselves from critical to compassionate allows us to grieve and slowly begin to reconcile our and our parent's losses. We may not be able to change the situation we are facing with our aging parents. But we can afford ourselves permission to be human and every opportunity to come to terms with the unwelcome reality.

"Doesn't do me any good to whine and cry about it," we finally say. "I've just got to deal with it."

That may sound like a good coping strategy. I've heard it more times than I could ever recall. But this quick-fix approach is not effective over time. Trying to reduce our pain, hiding from it, or denying and repressing sadness, only prolongs it—and the debt eventually comes due . . . with interest.

I invite you, and myself—yes, I also need reminders—to replace the voice of self-criticism, when it comes to working through our losses, with one of self-respect and self-compassion. My mantra of taking your foot off your throat and placing a hand over your heart, once again, gives you and me—each of us—the breathing room and permission we need to begin healing. Coming to terms with the living losses and setbacks that arise with our parents requires peaceful reconciliation.

"This really sucks!" we may say. "There's no doubt about it. I guess I don't get to play God—and despite my best efforts, I cannot control this situation. I've done the very best that I can and although I am very sad about the way things have turned out, I will somehow, somewhere, and in some way find the strength to go on. It is what it is!"

We will need that self-compassion, a touch of kindness and equanimity for where we're going next.

To deepen your understanding of the living losses that you, your parents and siblings may be experiencing, and a few tips on how to deal with them effectively, read my article on "Living Losses" on my website, www.kendruck.com.

Chapter 11

The Infinite Finality of Death

When my mother decided to move to California and we were looking for the right place for her to live, we visited a few senior living communities. As we toured around the facility checking out their amenities, it seemed that many of the residents weren't really "there." It was as though their minds were long gone and only their bodies remained. I wondered, were they simply waiting for the end? Would I be sending my mother to live in a place where people go to wait for the end? For the rest of the day, I couldn't shake the sadness of that thought.

Many of us are blindsided by the feelings that arise as we start to grapple with the end of life. The idea of losing our parents is, of course, heartbreaking. Even though we watch them get older, it's hard to imagine that their lives will one day end and that ours will somehow go on. Confronting death is unsettling, and some of the discomfort we feel in watching our parents' minds and bodies change has to do with our difficulty and unwillingness in coming to terms with our *own* mortality. We've been told that we will die someday, but we'd rather not acknowledge it. The decision to avoid dealing with our own impermanence leaves us ill-prepared to face the increasingly inescapable and undeniable reality that our parents' lives are winding down.

After touring a few more retirement communities, we ultimately chose the one that resonated with my mother's active senior lifestyle. She lived there quite happily, amid a new circle of friends. She even became the unofficial "mayor" of her community. But even the most active, high-spirited living environment cannot stave off the inevitable. Over time, my mother's mind and body began to slow down. Despite all the many ways she had managed to stay engaged with our family, her friends and the world, and tried to remain active, we knew she was struggling. And that the end of her life was slowly approaching.

The end of my mother's life came with little warning. Having lapsed into what we thought was a mini-stroke—a transient ischemic attack—she was taken to the hospital. Lisette and I rushed home from Indianapolis where I was giving a speech, as the West-Coast members of our family gathered at her bedside and the East-Coast family members boarded flights to come be with us. By the time we arrived at the hospital, my mother was unable to speak.

We were unsure whether she could hear or understand us, but our entire family continued to show her our love in every

The Infinite Finality of Death

possible way. Over the next few days, we transformed my mother's room at Scripps Hospital into a beautiful gathering place, putting on her favorite music, reminiscing and telling her how much we loved her. We also took night shifts, ensuring that a few of us would always be there—even sleeping in chairs by her bedside, in case she awakened, was in distress, or was nearing death. The hospital staff could not have been more loving or supportive of our family.

On the fifth day of her stay in the hospital, my mother's favorite song, "Somewhere Over the Rainbow" began to play on the CD that we had made. Spontaneously, we all moved in close and started serenading her. As we were singing my mother's favorite song, holding each other's hands, her grandchildren telling her "We love you Bubby!," my mother took her final breath. Her life had ended.

We all cried, held each other, kissed my mother, said a prayer for her to be at peace and even joked about what it would be like for her to see my father for the first time in thirty years. We all agreed that after a few moments of pure joy, they would probably find something to disagree about.

The last moments of life can be among the saddest and most terrifying we ever experience with our parents. And yet, they can also be some of the most sacred and loving.

> The last moments of life can be among the saddest and most terrifying we ever experience with our parents. And yet, they can also be some of the most sacred and loving.

Our parents do not live forever, and neither do we. Nor will our own children, favorite celebrities, friends, poets, pets or politicians. The terms and conditions of this life do, however, sometimes allow us to surround one another with inordinate amounts of love, care, compassion, grace, and gratitude during our days together and at the end of life.

Discovering What Our Parent Wants

While there may not be a way to prepare ourselves emotionally for the end of a parent's life, there are some things we can do to help ourselves. My mom was clear that she didn't want any "heroic measures" to be taken should she fall gravely ill. She did not want to be kept alive artificially. She just wanted to have her loved ones gathered around her at the end. To make sure she was not suffering. Be surrounded by our love. And be at peace that we would carry on in the way that she would want us to. To the best of our abilities, that's exactly what we did.

To the extent that your parent is willing to discuss these kinds of sensitive matters, do your best to find out what they want in their heart of hearts. What specifically do they want the end of their lives to look like?

In a perfect world, we would have an advance directive, or a living will, to minimize emergency end-of-life decision-making and trauma. We would know our parents' wishes. Also, we'd have a line of communication to their doctor, helping us see that their instructions are carried out. Thus, we would be able to honor their choices and minimize their suffering.

The Infinite Finality of Death

We don't live in that perfect world, so this is possible in some cases, and in others, it isn't. Our parent may not want to talk about it, and that's their choice.

As I mentioned earlier, knowing how daunting a challenge this can be for both aging parents and their adult children, my dear friend and visionary colleague, Rosemary Pahl, wrote *Departing Details Workbook: A Step-by-Step Guide to Leaving Your Loved Ones with the Information they Need to Know*. This wonderful workbook covers everything and has helped many thousands of families sort things out and avoid unnecessary pain and confusion.

There is also something of a revolution currently afoot regarding how we address these end-of-life questions. As a society, we're grappling with the concept of letting people decide for themselves what they want—in particular, regarding when they want to die. Societal views are shifting and laws are changing to reflect the notion that each of us gets to choose for ourselves when it's time, not unlike the way we discern that the quality of our beloved pet's life is so significantly diminished, and their suffering so great, that it's time to lovingly help them die.

We can expand our capacity for empathy and understanding during this process by taking a moment to think about what *we* might want. Ask yourself: "How do I want the final moments, hours, days, weeks, and months of my life to go?" Exploring this will let you step into your parents' shoes and then help them by asking the most difficult, yet important and appropriate questions about what they want.

If we are able to get a sense of what our parent genuinely wants, we can then do our best to help them make it a reality. As in any area of caring for an aging parent, the results probably won't be perfect. Nor do they need to be. We need to learn how to be at peace, by doing our best in life's most unspeakably difficult moments.

When They Pass

The rest of this chapter is devoted to exploring how we can honor our loved ones as we mourn their passing. Losing a parent may cause some of the most sorrowful moments of our lifetimes. The life of the person who not only gave us life, but also left us with a lifetime of good memories (hopefully), has come to an end.

If we have a surviving parent, we're probably surrounding them with a great deal of love, support and care as they grieve the loss of their partner. The many challenges of helping them plot out their future are just beginning and may often seem insurmountable.

It may also be the case that when a parent finally passes our predominant response is relief. We may experience sorrow and relief at the same time. These feelings often go hand in hand when a parent has suffered or became a living loss to us years before their physical death. We may even experience the loss of a dream we have secretly held since childhood, such as hearing a declaration of love or pride from our mother or father.

The Infinite Finality of Death

One fifty-four-year-old client told me that in the aftermath of his dad's memorial service, he felt he wasn't just burying his dad but was burying any chance that his father might miraculously turn into a more loving father who was proud of his son. "The hope that it will happen is now gone forever," my client said, "and I have to deal with that."

We may feel despair that our parent is gone, and relief because their suffering has come to an end. There is a deep meaning to the common phrase, "Rest in peace." Whether our parents' lives have been short, turbulent, and painful or long, peaceful, and satisfying, we may find a measure of comfort in the possibility that they are now at peace. Regardless of how we may view the afterlife, the idea that our parents' suffering has ended can bring us comfort.

It is crucially important to clear a path so we can make peace with the past and give our parents the full measure of our love, gratitude, and care in their final years.

A dear friend of mine recently recounted, "It's taken me years to realize I really didn't appreciate my mother while she was alive. Listening to the list of everything my girlfriend was grateful for at her mom's celebration of life, it finally hit me that I had done little more than tolerate my mother. That same night, I had a dream that I was running around like a maniac, desperately trying to find my mom so I could read her my list of gratitude. I have finally realized how much I valued what she gave me, how much she really loved me and how much I love her. Forgiving myself for how caught up I was in my own world that I missed telling my mother how grateful I was . . . has been difficult. But it's what she would want, so I will continue to work at it."

Expressing your gratitude, communicating your love, "forgiving" your parents for not being perfect, asking them what they want as they get older, and forgiving yourself for those times you were too caught up in your own life to notice theirs is how you can begin to make peace.

Honoring Them Through a Memorial Service

Our parent's memorial service is a chance for us to bless their life and take another step forward in making peace. Whether this heavy subject is part of the distant past, too far into the future to think about, or happening at this very moment, it is worth taking more than a few minutes of your time to consider.

Losing a parent is an inescapably painful and often chaotic time. The memorial service allows us to honor the value of what the parent accomplished, acknowledge the struggles the mother or father faced, and—if it's in keeping with who the parent was—share a joke and a laugh. In this way, we celebrate the totality of their life.

My mom used to love a good debate, but as she got older, she just couldn't argue the way she used to. She also didn't want to waste the time we had together by having petty disagreements. So what did my brilliant, somewhat competitive, and conflict-avoidant mother do? She invented a new strategy

The Infinite Finality of Death

called "case closed." If she felt that she was losing an argument, she would say, "All right, *case closed*." When we heard that phrase, we knew the conversation had been declared over by executive decree.

A year before my mother passed, we were visiting the cemetery where my dad and daughter are buried. Telling me how much she liked my father's headstone, she asked, "Can you help me design a headstone for me *and* your father?" And so, the following week, I took my mom headstone shopping.

After picking one out and creating the inscriptions for both my father and mother's sides of the stone, she asked if we could put something at the bottom of her inscription, that was similar to my father's, which said, "Whose Everlasting Love and Generosity Endures." We both broke out into loud laughter when we knew what to put below the words, "Loving mother and grandmother." Yes, you guessed it. The bottom of my mother's side of the headstone reads, "Case Closed."

Grieving in a Grief-Illiterate Culture

Many years after the tragic death of Princess Diana, CNN asked me to appear on a program with her sons, Prince William and Prince Harry. At that time, the United Kingdom was in the midst of an initiative to improve understanding and compassion around mental health issues, and part of that undertaking was a dialogue about grief. Having endured my own tragedy and spent a good part of my adult life helping others through devastating losses, I had become a trusted expert and was frequently asked to help the general public after a disaster or tragedy.

Both William and Harry had decided they were finally ready to talk about how their mother's death had affected them. They said that, at first, they had tried to avoid dealing with the loss. In fact, the entire royal family had tried to spin and speed their way through grief and loss. Both princes explained that they had tried to be good Brits by keeping a stiff upper lip—so they had hidden and suppressed their feelings.

But the truth, they shared, was that after their mother's death, they were shattered. With time, they had realized there was nothing wrong with them for feeling this sense of deep sorrow and confusion about what had happened and how their lives had been changed forever. They had endured an unspeakable tragedy, and what they felt in its wake was horrific. How could they not feel these things? And how could they possibly survive now without inordinate amounts of love, understanding, support, and permission to be young boys who had just lost their mother?

On international television with William and Harry, I spoke openly about the limits and dangers of living in grief-illiterate cultures. As part of our cultural avoidance of death, it is common for many people to put a positive spin on our losses. While we're grieving, those around us often feel a pressure to try and remove our sorrow, rather than find ways to support us as we experience it.

The Infinite Finality of Death

Don't get me wrong; the support we get in our time of need can be a blessing. But even well-intentioned family members, friends, and coworkers can say deeply insensitive or irrelevant things. Or they can resort to useless clichés like, "God needed another angel," "Everything works out for the best," and "They're in a better place now." Their aim, however misguided, is to fix us or make us feel better by taking away our sadness and pain and also ease their own discomfort with not knowing how to respond to our grief.

Indeed, in our culture there seems to an abiding belief that there's a fix for every problem, a diversion for every moment of emptiness, and a pill for every pain. On that CNN broadcast with Prince William and Prince Harry, I affirmed the importance of giving ourselves permission to be human, to grieve, and to honor those we have lost in the way we live on.

Sometimes life asks us to stand tall in our moments of sorrow and despair because that is our true experience. Reaching for some sort of religious, psychological, or spiritual quick fix may provide a temporary relief. But we soon discover its limits. And if we truly pass through the experience of grief, what we may find is a fullness behind the emptiness, a "found-ness" behind the "lost-ness" a feeling of wholeness that arises from allowing that part of ourselves to be broken. Summoning the strength, courage, and faith to turn the love that became sorrow back into resilient love is one of life's great miracles. Having worked with countless bereaved individuals and families, and having found a path to healing after the loss of my daughter Jenna, I developed a road map I want to share with you.

The Six Honorings

Loss changes us. We are different now, as Barbara Kingsolver so eloquently expressed in that passage I mentioned in the last chapter: "You don't think you'll live past it. And you don't, really. The person you were is gone."

So how do we live on? How do we keep from letting our despair become the central organizing principle of our lives? In answer to these questions, I have created something called the Six Honorings. Together, these six steps are a gentle guide for living with loss and offering homage to the one we loved and lost.

The First Honoring: Survive the death of those you love.

The first way that we honor those we've lost is to survive their death. We allow ourselves to mourn, acknowledging that grieving a loss is as natural and normal as bleeding when we're cut. We take care of ourselves. We show ourselves care and compassion. And, somehow, we summon the strength to survive.

The Second Honoring: Do something good in their name.

You may choose to do something as simple and elegant as lighting a candle or planting a tree, or as elaborate as building something in their honor. Recently, I've been working with several families who lost children to addiction, and the parents are responding by speaking out about the pandemic of addiction in this country. In this way, they are doing a good in the name of the one they lost.

The Third Honoring: Cultivate a spiritual relationship with your loved ones.
We used to be able to pop over for a visit or pick up the phone and hear their voice. Now, we know we aren't going to see or hear them again—at least, not in the way we always did. That's why the Third Honoring is to begin to cultivate a spiritual relationship with them. I continue to say out loud, "How's my favorite mother today?" the way I used to, when she was alive. By continuing to talk to her, I am affirming that the love never dies and that we can continue to give and receive love in a spiritual way.

The Fourth Honoring: Embody an element of their spirit.
Whether it is their love, enthusiasm, kindness, sense of humor, or even their irreverence, choose a beautiful, eternal aspect of their spirit, and begin to embody it. "I'm going to be more *that* way when I grow up," we say to ourselves as kids, and then we cultivate that quality in our lives.

The Fifth Honoring: Write new chapters of life.
This honoring is the most challenging. To the best of our ability, we work to live out the rest of our lives as an expression of our love. We do not allow ourselves to dwell in the torture

chamber of guilt, obsessing over what could have or should have happened. Rather than beating ourselves up for what we didn't do, we keep in mind the ways we were a good son or daughter. We celebrate the things that went well. We count the blessings that we brought into our parents' lives: our love and care, the joyful times we had together, and possibly even the grandchildren we gave them. And we forgive ourselves for the ways we might have done better. We may also have missed the opportunity to express gratitude for these blessings, but now they are gone, and it's on us. We acknowledge the ways we were good children to them. We count the blessings we gave them and the ones they gave us. And then we find new ways of living our lives and making new memories as an expression of that love.

The Sixth Honoring: Take the high road.

With many families who were torn apart in the rawness of grief after 9/11, we started a program called, "Take the High Road." We agreed to treat one another with patience, kindness, respect, humility, compassion, and understanding as an expression of our love for the person who had died. Rather than allowing the dark aspects of grief to destroy our families, close friendships, schools, companies, and communities, we would take the high road and appeal to each other's "better angels."

The Resurfacing of Conflict

When a parent dies, some of the most difficult family conflicts may resurface. Even if all the siblings are able to cooperate to

The Infinite Finality of Death

some degree when managing a parent's care, the parent's passing may bring an end to the peace. As I warned earlier, once-dormant sibling rivalries can arise seemingly out of nowhere.

The rawness of emotions at the end of a parents' life, along with sorting out the myriad of things that need to be done as part of winding down a parent's affairs, can unleash the best or the very worst in us and our families. We may find ourselves in a state of mind where we're so hypersensitive, defensive and hurt that we take up arms against other family members. As the shock of actually losing a parent wears off, the flood of emotions that come with it can lead us to spew repressed pain, anger, and/or jealousy with reckless abandon. The intensity of these emotions can damage sibling relationships at a time when you need each other's love, patience, understanding and support more than ever.

In one family I helped, the mother died and left behind three daughters, each with a very different personality. One daughter was responsible, and so her mom had selected her to handle the estate and all her affairs. The mother had also asked this oldest daughter to handle a piece of property she owned and made her the executor.

"You're the only one that comes to visit me," she has told her. "Maybe I should give it to you. Or your sisters can buy you out." Alas, the mother never talked with her other two daughters about this decision.

When the mom's health eventually failed and she died, a war broke out between the sisters. Because the mother had not settled any of her affairs in advance, the two younger sisters began to act out all the jealousy, resentment, and injustice they'd felt toward their big sister. One of them actually snuck into their mother's empty condo at night and took a truckload of belongings. When the older sister arranged to sell the condo, the other two banded together and accused her of cheating them. Things got very ugly. After the condo was sold and the funds were distributed evenly to each daughter, the sisters stopped communicating with one another.

As bad as this situation was, it wasn't unusual. Families often disintegrate into distrust when a deceased parent's material and financial assets become the currency of their love. Children are ostensibly fighting over money or possessions—*"I want that lamp!"*—but they may truly be fighting for the last claim on love, attention, and special status from their mother.

There are a couple of things we can do to avoid this kind of nightmare from occurring in our families.

The "Take the High Road" Program

As I shared earlier, it's critically important to set the right tone within the family before irreparable damage is done to sibling relationships. After a loss, everyone is in the rawness of grief. In the midst of this period of heightened sensitivity, the things people say and do can be deeply hurtful and upend relationships and the entire family system. Being especially

> After a loss, everyone is in the rawness of grief. Being especially mindful of what we all say and do is critical.

The Infinite Finality of Death

mindful of what we all say and do is critical. Being as patient and forgiving as possible, listening to our siblings, and asking open-ended questions of them, is the secret to keeping the peace.

After 9/11, when I helped create support groups for those who had lost loved ones in and around New York and in California. At that time, we noticed a pattern in the type of conflict that was arising within families. The average age of the victims of 9/11 was thirty-eight, which in most cases meant the deceased person had a young family as well as a living mother and father. But the government was typically communicating only with the deceased person's spouse. That meant there were grieving parents who were basically left out of the loop—and who therefore, in many cases, became incensed that all the attention and communication was directed at their son's or daughter's spouse. "He was my son!" they cried in pain. "She was my daughter!"

We have all heard beautiful stories of love and sacrifice that unfolded in the rawness following those traumatic deaths. Bruce Springsteen's anthemic song, "The Rising" speaks of these things. But there were also horrific wars erupting within families. Young widows who were shunned by their in-laws retaliated by keeping children away from their grandparents. Threats such as, "You're never going to see your grandkids again," began tearing families apart. We needed to do something.

I created the Take the High Road program to show family members that they had a choice. They could allow the darkness and despair of what had happened to tear them and their families apart, or they could summon understanding and patience to show one another a path back into the light by moving forward in life. At the core of the program materials I wrote and ideas I shared was a simple ethic to treat your family members as an expression of your love for the person who died. I facilitated dozens of Family Counsel Meetings helping family members speak to and treat one another as their lost loved one would want. Permanent damage could be done to 9/11 families who allowed themselves to be splintered by anger. But we could rise above the pain.

The basic tenets of Take the High Road, a program I still offer, are fairly simple:

- Speak in kind tones.
- Show compassion, because the other person is hurting just like you.
- Don't judge! Everyone is trying to get through this in his or her own way.
- Be patient—if a family member lashes out at you, don't jump into the fire with him or her. Apologize quickly if you screw up and say or do something hurtful. As best you can, try not to let yourself get defensive. Listen and stay humble! Avoid getting caught up in old family dramas, grudges, and jealousies.
- Practice self-care by telling people, "This is not a good time for me to discuss/do/deal with that. Can we please take that up at a later time?" Do not try to settle family differences or make big family decisions. Go one breath, one day at a time.

The Infinite Finality of Death

When family members choose to take the high road, they come together in a way that affords them every opportunity to heal as a family and honor the deceased.

"I Hope the Day Goes Gently for You"

The first weeks and months of grief are a rollercoaster. Your parent is gone, and in all likelihood, you're feeling completely heartsick. You can't pick up the phone and call Mom anymore. You can't go visit Dad any longer. The fact that life will never be the same is sinking in as you go back and forth from surreal to all too real.

When I encounter people dealing with such deep sorrow, I have learned simply to say, "I am so sorry for your loss" and "I hope the day goes gently for you."

If you are reading this book at a time of loss, may it be so for you.

Chapter 12

Managing Your Own Needs in the Second Half of Life

You may have heard it a hundred times while waiting for a flight to take off, and you may have heard it another hundred times as a cliché: "Put on your own oxygen mask before helping others." So maybe you've heard it two hundred times, but the wisdom in that bit of advice is as true now as the first time it was spoken, because we can't effectively help others until we've taken care of ourselves. Giving ourselves care—balancing rest and activity, setting healthy boundaries, clarifying the terms and conditions of our involvement, and knowing how and when to unplug and rejuvenate—allows us to give care to others.

Each chapter of this book has emphasized the importance of taking care of ourselves in one way or another, but this chapter goes further. In the next few pages, you'll find key information about what I call "professional-grade self-care."

We may be experts at pampering ourselves. Getting a regular mani/pedi, watching *The Late Show with Stephen Colbert*, and/or enjoying an açai bowl breakfast might be part of your routine. Some of us are even in the health-care profession. Yet when it comes to taking five minutes—never mind an hour—to take care of ourselves, most of us get poor marks.

My good friend, Dr. Spencer Johnson, author of *Who Moved My Cheese*, understands that learning to sit quietly and breathe, kicking back and putting our feet up, or just saying, "No" may be really hard for many of us. It's what prompted him to write *One Minute for Yourself* many years ago. Spencer also inspired me to write *The Self-Care* Handbook, which has evolved into a training program I offer to professionals working in healthcare, law enforcement, financial services, domestic violence advocacy, and the military.

We may have spent our entire lives thinking that there's something indisputably noble in sacrificing our own needs in favor of others' needs, and doing so at any cost. Many of us have mastered caregiving to the point of being self-sacrificing martyrs, tireless pleasers, family heroes, and even "saints." And most of us tend to justify sacrificing a disproportionate amount of our time, health, and energy at work making a living.

There are few areas of life more demanding of care than our family relationships. The challenges of taking care of ourselves as our parents age can be as challenging as the ones parents face when their children are very young. The seemingly never-ending needs of both young children and aging parents can be draining and exhausting.

It's never too early or too late to build mastery in the area of self-care. The challenges we face as caregivers for aging parents make it essential. Maybe we have routines of going to the gym three days a week, decompressing in front of the television during "happy hour," or sleeping late on weekends—routines that have worked well for us in the past but that we now find are not nearly enough.

As we all know, it isn't easy to change. The old way of getting things done is deeply ingrained in us. Improving in our self-care requires making a new commitment to ourselves to push past our existing comfort zone and acquire some new tools and habits. Before we take a look here at the key tenets of professional-grade, self-care, let's consider the most common and troublesome saboteurs and stumbling that keep us from caring for ourselves and result in a severe form of burnout that I call Caregiving Fatigue Syndrome, or CFS.

> Improving in our self-care requires making a new commitment to ourselves to push past our existing comfort zone and acquire some new tools and habits.

All That Stands in Our Way

First and foremost, such professional-grade self-care requires newfound permission to attend to our own needs. Old habits can stand in the way of allowing us to do the very things that are necessary to really take care of ourselves. When we don't question those habits, we continue to deny ourselves the love, care, and respect we need. Here are a few self-defeating behaviors to consider when assessing and overcoming your resistance to change.

Excuses, excuses, excuses

Excuses top the list of subtle, but effective, ways we justify inaction, procrastination, passive resistance, outright refusal, and half-hearted attempts at self-care. There are endless (and sometimes genuinely good) reasons we cannot take time out for ourselves. We justify inaction by telling ourselves and others we don't have time, are unsure of what to do with our kids, are worried we might lose our jobs . . . it's a long list. Take one minute to lie on a yoga mat and stretch. Walk the dog down to the corner. Or just listen to one song you love. It may be hard to see how you can afford to do this, but now is the time to realize you cannot afford *not* to. Replace excuses with small, simple acts of self-care.

Being in an abusive or controlling relationship

The best among us sometimes mistakenly end up in hostile or even abusive relationships that hold us back from loving, respecting, and caring for ourselves. In such relationships, an act of self-care or independence is considered a threat. Accused of being perceived as selfish or spoiled, we defer and throw ourselves under the proverbial bus. We allow the needs of a controlling partner, supervisor, or parent to prevail, all the while ignoring our own needs. This can cause us to feel helpless and undeserving, and we may work our way into a deep depression.

Allowing guilt, shame, fear, and embarrassment to shut us down

Some of us are prone to feeling guilty. This is especially true when another person we know is unhappy or upset, and we feel we're responsible. We may both blame ourselves when things don't go perfectly and shame ourselves for feeling good when they do. Embarrassment, guilt, and shame of this kind are self-defeating. And they cripple us when it comes to practicing self-care. We need and deserve care—and must summon the strength and courage to finally free ourselves of the things that hold us back from giving it.

Feeling unworthy/undeserving

Some of us simply do not feel deserving or worthy of love, care, respect, or affection. The idea of taking time just for ourselves is unthinkable. We might have been brought up to believe it's our job to tend to everyone else's needs and automatically disallow our own. Or we grew up thinking poorly of ourselves and therefore as punishment, we deny ourselves the love, care, support, and attention we need. Not surprisingly, we end up spending much of our time alone as victims, not having communicated our true wants, needs, or preferences.

Perfectionism

Having internalized the belief that perfection is required, we strive for it in everything we do, from parenting to how we appear. We can never do enough to satisfy our boss, parents, or children, and therefore we think we don't deserve to take time out for resting, rewarding, replenishing, rebalancing, or simply loving ourselves. "Do more, more, more!" is our mantra. Working ourselves into a state of exhaustion, habitually running on empty tanks, we become susceptible to burnout, depression, and psychosomatic illness. As my son-in-law, Tony, reminds me, "Don't let the perfect be the enemy of the good."

Fear of losing status, power, and identity

In some cultures, including those created within businesses, self-care is seen as self-indulgent, weak, or shameful. It's no different in many of our families. Long-suffering behaviors, including lack of sleep and food deprivation, excessive overwork, passive neglect of one's health, and martyrdom become signs of strength, loyalty, and noble sacrifice. Whether we're acting this way for our parents, the team, or the company, we allow our fear of losing status to be the controlling factor in how—or even if—we take care of ourselves. When we allow our fears to shape our decisions about taking a much-needed break, our behavior is the antithesis of good health and well-being. Once again, breaking free of these self-limiting fears will allow us to think clearly about how to take good care of ourselves and then actually do so.

Unforgiving, self-defeating, and self-punishing behavior
Although it's not always easy to see or admit, sometimes we have it out for ourselves. That's right; we become our own worst enemy. When we're at war with ourselves, there's little or no possibility for self-love or self-care. Punishing, berating, and beating ourselves up for something we did or failed to do in the past is a kind of self-defeating retribution or payback. It's as if we're in a courtroom with only a prosecuting attorney. With no lawyer representing us, or impartial judge or jury to weigh our case, we are virtually defenseless against our own accusations. Acting this way, we make circumstances harder and more painful than they need to be. Those of us who fall into this self-destructive pattern of turning opportunities for self-care into episodes of self-neglect often end up portraying ourselves as victims. And yet, ironically, it is by our own hand that we are suffering. Take a moment to just think about some of the other ways you allow things to stand in the way of becoming a more self-caring individual? Now, try to be conscious of these tendencies as you move ahead.

The Seven Keys to Self-Care

We've now looked at the things that keep us from truly taking care of ourselves. But awareness of our demons and saboteurs alone will not be enough to free us from old patterns. Your willingness to take positive action when you feel yourself slipping into a pattern of self-neglect or indifference is critical to making lasting changes in the way you think and act. It takes time, patience, and persistence, in order to stave off the discouragement, setbacks, and regression under stress that are, in fact, part of the growing process. Whether you are the caregiving son, daughter, or grandchild of an aging parent, here are seven powerful tools for cultivating the kind of self-care that will allow you to be at your best:

Key #1: Make the decision to change the way you care for yourself.

Undertaking change of this magnitude and importance takes courage, humility, conviction, and a new and improved vision of your best future. These ingredients allow us to say "Yes!" to ourselves. We have a right to do the things that make life better, easier, less stressful, and more joyful. We also have a right to say "No" to the people and things that drain and deplete us, including members of our own family. Sustainable change requires a promise to ourselves to do whatever is necessary to become the more self-caring, self-respecting version of ourselves. We may not know exactly how we're going to change, but we're committed to finding out and doing what's necessary starting right now.

Key #2: Define your end goal.

Begin to sketch out what you want your life to look and feel like after you have succeeded. Perhaps you're feeling happier, sleeping longer, exercising regularly, eating better, and speaking to yourself with greater kindness and compassion. You might have taken on a role in your family or just with your aging parents that needs to be rebalanced. Or you have been a lifelong pleaser who is finally ready to face your own fears about letting people down, feeling worthless, or being alone. Some of us have gotten used to following the elephant around the circus with a shovel, and we are just now waking up. Something is shifting inside of us, declaring, "Enough! It's time to put down the shovel!" We are ripe for a change. You may even be ready to hand in your resignation as someone's doormat, whipping post, dumping ground, enabler, or damage control in favor of a healthier, more reciprocal caregiving relationship. Whatever your end goal, take the time to define it in clear, practical terms. Get concrete about your desired outcome by writing it down.

Key #3: Make a list of people and things you need to say "No" to.

Although this book has focused on fine-tuning your relationship with your family of origin, write down the names of at least five people you need to take better care of yourself with and learn how to say "No" to. Begin each sentence with, "A person I need to learn how to say 'No' to is…" or "I need to learn how to say 'No' when or because…" or "The benefits of saying 'No' are . . ." Those of us who've spent a good part of our lives taking care of other people's needs say "Yes" almost automatically when asked. We volunteer ourselves without giving much, if any, consideration to our own health and sanity. It's time to stop putting ourselves at risk and spreading ourselves thin by overcommitting our time and energy. Prioritizing and saying "No" may be painfully hard in the beginning, especially if it involves an aging parent. Old feelings of guilt, obligation and responsibility are hard to kick. After a while, however, you will begin to feel the benefits of self-care and thank yourself for staying strong. The people who matter will still love you and the ones who depended on you to say "Yes" even when it wasn't in your best interest will probably complain and play the abandoned victim. They will also become somebody else's problem. The results of learning to say "No"—and of delegating shared responsibility among your siblings, coworkers, and any caregivers you employ to help your parent—will speak for themselves.

Key #4: Lighten your load, unburden yourself, and allow pleasure.

If you've spent years training the people around you that with a little guilt, a warm smile, or an angry glance, you'll do anything, it's time to begin letting folks know you're in the process of making a change. Learning to tune out and replace the voice of inner guilt with one of reason and self-compassion takes time and practice, like any new skill, and you may receive some uncomfortable pushback while you're doing it. On the other hand, you may also be surprised by the patience, kindness, encouragement, and support you get as you learn to delegate and share responsibility with others.

Managing Your Own Needs in the Second Half of Life

The most self-critical voice you contend with may be in your own mind—one that tells you that you absolutely can't say "No" to someone else and say "Yes" to yourself. Don't let the old voices of self-criticism and condemnation weaken your resolve, as they once did, to turn off the computer and take a hot bath. Practice doing the very things that lighten your heart and your load. Set yourself free to nurture, pamper, and care for yourself. Allow, delight in, and savor the stress-free sides of life. Give yourself permission, encouragement, and the ability to lighten up, let go and be happy!

Key #5: Listen to yourself.

Sometimes the best source of wise counsel about self-care comes from deep within. Tuning in to the gentler inner voice that tells us to slow down, relax, or take it easy can give us the encouragement, strength, and guidance we need to take care of ourselves. Listening to the kindest, most nurturing parts of ourselves that say, "It's okay!" is a self-care mantra many of us can use to free ourselves from the feeling that we can never do or be enough for our aging parents. As I have shared several times in this book, learning to quiet your mind, often by placing your hand on your own hearts, is key.

Key #6: Find a self-care opportunity in every one of your relationships.

The choices we make in our relationships are a reflection of our willingness and ability to practice self-care. Relationships are one of life's greatest testing grounds for learning reciprocity. Finding and maintaining balance in taking care of ourselves while tending to our relationships—with family, aging parents, kids, friends, and coworkers—is one of life's greatest challenges. It is also a place where we can create unlimited opportunities to free ourselves of unrelenting self-care saboteurs and practice taking better care of ourselves.

Key #7: Pat yourself on the back for a job well done.

When it comes to taking better care of yourself, every step forward—even a baby step—is worthy of an encouraging pat on the back. You did it! Despite the fear and resistance that comes with change, you are summoning the courage and strength to become a better, more self-caring version of yourself. This is deep and difficult work, not something to take for granted or gloss over. Stop and think about one thing you're doing to take better care of yourself. Progress is progress. With every ounce of generosity and self-appreciation you can muster, quiet your mind and give yourself a well-deserved pat on the back.

Your Self-Care Master Plan

It's time to put all of this into concrete action. The changes that lead to exceptional results are born here, in what will become your Self-Care Master Plan. What you stipulate in each of the categories listed below will define what you must now do. Please write down what you're willing to do, step by step, to take better care of yourself in the moments, days, weeks, months, and years ahead. You may choose to focus on the self-care challenges you have with your aging parents and siblings, or the ones you have in general. It's your call. Make this investment in yourself, your health, and your future. You're worth it! Below, I have provided a few sample actions to help you get started in thinking about your own plan. Please be concrete, specific, and realistic.

SELF-CARE MASTER PLAN

Psychological Self-Care

Sample Actions:

- I will catch myself when speaking in a self-deprecating/critical tone.
- I will practice speaking to myself with kindness.
- I will work on disempowering my saboteurs, especially guilt.
- I will keep a "You're worth it!" sign on my desk.
- I will meditate, walk in nature, and listen to relaxing music.

My Plan:

- _____
  _____
  _____
  _____
  _____

Physical Self-Care

Sample Actions:

- I will schedule two self-care stretch breaks in each day.
- I will begin walking/hiking/swimming/taking yoga classes every other day.
- I will get nutritional coaching and lose a recommended number of pounds by next year at this time.
- I will schedule regular health checkups with my doctor and dentist.

My Plan:

- _____

_____

Relationship/Family Self-Care

Sample Actions:

- I will say "No" to Mom or Dad when the time, situation, or terms are not right.
- I will make time to nurture and replenish my marriage.
- I will limit the time I spend with people who drain me.
- I will clear the air of conflict with people I care about.

My Plan:

- _____

_____

_____

Work Self-Care

Sample Actions:

- I will tell my boss I'm no longer going to work before 8:30 a.m. or past 5:30 p.m.
- I will become a better communicator with my co-workers.
- I will begin to more effectively delegate and share responsibility with my coworkers.
- I will talk to my supervisor about my future position and pay.

My Plan:

- _____

_____

Spiritual Self-Care

Sample Actions:

- I will read about and attend talks/workshops on spiritual deepening.
- I will take time to attend religious services and deepen my faith.
- I will spend more time with friends who value spiritual awareness.
- I will allow myself more time in silence, solitude, and prayer.

My Plan:

- _____

_____

Other Self-Care

Sample Actions:

- I will take quiet time every day after work to decompress.
- I will play soft, soothing music each day.
- I will not to take on any more school, work, neighborhood, or community projects for the rest of the year.
- I will redo my "bucket list" to reflect more of my own true needs.
- I will get the help I need but have avoided, especially in regard to my parents.

My Plan:

- _____
  _____
  _____
  _____

To create your own **Self-Care Master Plan**, you can download a free copy or use The *Raising an Aging Parent Personal Journal*, available for purchase at www.kendruck.com. Keep it where you can see it and add to it as you become aware of new ways you can take care of yourself. Share it with trusted family members, friends, advocates, confidants, and colleagues whose support can help you follow up on the commitments you have made to yourself. Remember that this plan is a working document designed to change your life for the better.

It may also be the single most important guide to determining the quality of your life and allowing you to be the very best son or daughter to your aging parent. And it may be a wonderful source of inspiration for your siblings, cousins, and friends who are also searching for ways to take better care of themselves with their aging parents. Do not hide it away where it will accumulate dust. Post it where you can see it, put it to use, bring about change, and thrive!

> Self-care may also be the single most important guide to determining the quality of your life and allowing you to be the very best son or daughter to your aging parent.

A Prayer—and a Work in Progress

As I have said before, self-care is like placing a hand over your own heart, literally and metaphorically. And taking your foot off of your throat, my favorite expression for refraining from harsh self-criticism. Giving yourself what should be yours has nothing to do with selfishness or entitlement. Rather, it is a gift born of a humble gratitude for the life you have been given and appreciation for the person you are. While it's great to have a master plan and an end goal, self-care is a work in progress. Don't wait until a crisis or the end of life to grant yourself permission for loving care.

My wish for you, in whichever stage or season of life you happen to be, is to cultivate life-affirming, health-giving self-care practices. May the gentleness, kindness, self-compassion, generosity of heart, forgiveness, permission, and peace you're learning to give yourself spread like a warm breeze across the bow of your family, community and the world.

In the final chapter of this book we will explore the ways that taking care of ourselves and caring for an aging parent builds strong family bonds and pays forward the best in us to future generations.

Chapter 13

Leaving a Legacy of Love: Creating the Best Possible Future

At first glance, the title of this chapter may seem like too much to promise or imagine. Given what we've been through—all the changes, losses, turns in the road—how, we may ask, could we dare to believe in creating our best possible future by leaving a legacy of love in our family? And might doing this have any positive effect on the troubled world we live in?

As you'll see, everything that you've read about and worked toward in the previous chapters has paved the way to a better life for you and for your aging parents. A happy family is not one that is carefree, without conflict or loss. Life doesn't work that way. On the contrary, a happy family is one in which its members have learned that life is a package deal. We savor the joys, gifts, blessings, adventures, and miracles our lives have afforded us, and we do our resilient best to turn into opportunities for growth all of life's inescapable and unwelcome conflicts, disappointments, losses, changes, and growing pains, including the ones that come with raising an aging parent.

Family relationships are complicated. The fact that most families are riddled with conflict is a testament to how challenging relationships between aging parents and their adult children can be. It's hard being a human being and even harder interacting with others. That's difficult! And yet we think something's wrong when differences and problems arise. In fact, these "hiccups" are simply part of the nature of relationships and being a family.

Bear in mind that we're all making life up as we live it. It's not as though our parents raised several sets of "starter kids," so that when we arrived they knew exactly how to raise us. They didn't always know what to do, but they used what they had and did the best they could, just as we're doing with our own children and aging parents. Everyone makes mistakes, and differences will inevitably arise between members of any family. Sorting out those differences in a loving, constructive way is what makes a family whole. We learn to bridge our differences in the safety of a loving framework called a family.

As parents age, there will be undeniable pain that comes with love. When I work with families grieving the loss of a parent, I sometimes offer them two choices. The first is this: "In order to stop feeling this terrible sorrow, you must sever all the nerves to your emotional heart, and stop loving your mother or father." The second choice is different. "Bear the pain of this loss to keep your love alive forever," it begins. "Endure these tidal waves of grief knowing that your love for them will live on."

No one has ever chosen the first option.

But know there will be pain with the second. Since this is a given, the best we can do is prepare ourselves to weather the storms and tidal waves when they come. Every grief has a life and timetable all its own. Allowing ourselves to mourn the losses of our parents and generously permitting ourselves a period of sorrow is how we find the strength to continue living out our own lives.

> Allowing ourselves to mourn the losses of our parents and generously permitting ourselves a period of sorrow is how we find the strength to continue living out our own lives.

In each chapter of this book, we have covered different aspects of how to be resilient and build stronger bonds as a family. Those lessons both give us a deeper understanding of how to love an aging parent and provide us with powerful insights into how families move through the cycle of life and make the most of their time together.

Heartfelt Guidelines for a Healthy Family in the Second Half of Life

Yes, watching our parents get older is hard. And losing them is heartbreaking. Whether or not you're going through a loss right now, trying to build strength in anticipation of the inevitable, or wanting to make sure you are doing all you can to care for a parent, here are a few final suggestions. The following agreements, practices and guidelines, summarizing what we've learned about effectively raising an aging parent, can help us navigate the uncertain future, and harvest the love we have for others. Check the boxes of the guidelines, practices and agreements below that will make your relationships and our world a kinder, safer, and better place:

- We agree to communicate our needs and wants in a direct, forthright, and respectful manner.
- We agree to get out in front of potential family conflicts by talking things out, listening to one another, and setting healthy limits and boundaries.
- We agree to operate in good faith, giving others the benefit of the doubt.
- We agree to remain humble and apologize if/when appropriate.
- We agree to clarify how we feel and what we really want.
- We agree to work through family disagreements and make collaborative decisions when possible.
- We agree to let go of anger and resentment and to forgive one another.
- We agree to take good care of ourselves and one another during stressful periods.

Leaving a Legacy of Love: Creating the Best Possible Future

- We agree to keep our hearts open to each other.
- We agree to get help from a family coach/counselor if and when we reach an impasse, get stuck in conflict or go through a tragedy.
- We agree to keep one another in the loop when it comes to making family-related decisions.
- We agree to embrace "enough-ness" by acknowledging that we aren't perfect, that we don't live in a perfect world, that we won't do a perfect job as the adult children of aging parents, and that our parents weren't perfect parents to us but that they did their best, just as we are doing.
- We agree to try to make peace with life as it is. When we experience the pain of our parents changing or diminishing right before our eyes, we grieve a living loss. Realizing that our parents are not going to be with us forever, we tap into and voice the unspoken, unexpressed love, gratitude, forgiveness and appreciation we have for them. And when they pass, we grieve the conclusion of their lives, as well as the parts of our own lives that have now come to an end. By learning to allow our sorrow and discovering how intricately connected it is to our love, we begin to navigate a new era of our spiritual journey through this life.
- We agree that we are works in progress as a family and that our fears, anger, and insecurities will sometimes get the better of us. In these times, we will do our best to

take a deep breath, get back on track, follow guidelines like these and forgive ourselves and one another when and wherever necessary.

By following these guidelines, cultivating these practices, and working hard to keep these agreements, we make it more likely that our relationships with our parents and siblings will go well. At the core of successful relationships between aging parents and adult children are conversations they need to have with one another. For adult children, this starts with listening to things your parents might like to tell you but have not worked up the courage or trust to do so. Summoning the strength to talk to your parents about what's in your heart is paramount. With patience and love, ask open-ended questions such as, "Mom, what makes your heart sing? And what makes it heavy?"

Raising an aging parent is a call to step up in new and powerfully caring ways; to take on a new role in our lives, balance the care we are giving to someone else with the care we give ourselves, and make a few midcourse adjustments in how we view our parents. It's time to pay forward the good in our lives, including the fairness, kindness, forgiveness, directness, and courage we have cultivated in our families.

Whether you're a member of the sandwich generation, caring for your aging parents and kids at the same time and trying to have a life of your own, or you're in the busiest time of your life, chaotic yet also rich with meaning, or you're in the emptiest, loneliest season of your life, devoid of activity and purpose, do your best to rise to the occasion. Bear down, show up, and make some changes for the better.

Decide what you'd most like to change, and then make it happen. If you're the kind of person who pushes too hard for change in family matters, lighten up. And if you're the kind of person who doesn't push hard enough for change, push a little harder.

Finding Peace

Imagine you're having coffee or lunch with a dear friend, one who knows what you went through with your parents. Candidly, your friend asks, "How do you feel about what happened with your parents and in your family?"

Your answer may be one of pride, satisfaction, and joy about the way things turned out. But it's also possible that you experienced deep hurt, despair, frustration, and resentment. Or you may answer that you feel a mixture of these things: happy your parents gave you and your siblings a wonderful childhood, but sad they are getting older. You may look squarely into the eyes of that dear friend and say, "You know what? Growing up with my dad was not easy, but I'm okay now."

Years ago, I flew to Chicago to see Ace, a close friend of mine who had been a Special Ops Marine and was now dying of ALS. Ace and I had very different political views but we loved each other dearly. In addition to the many ways he had been like a brother to me, Ace had been a godfather to my daughter Jenna. Along with my buddies Terry, Mark, and Robert, he was a lifeline to me in the agonizing days after Jenna's death, imploring me to keep on keeping on.

Before I left the hospital on that last visit, Ace gave me one of the greatest blessings of my life.

"Looks like you'll be the first to kiss Jenna," I said to him.

"You've still got to fly home tonight," he replied.

His message that life is uncertain, and that we should not take anything for granted, has stayed with me all these years. But his next words were the ones that became a blessing:

"Kenny, we did good!"

Though I had been in the presence of many great religious figures of our time, including Mother Teresa, the Pope, and the Dalai Lama, I felt that this blessing meant more to me than any other.

I wish the same blessing for you. May each of us someday look back on the landscape of our lives and say, "Given all the surprises, unwelcome changes and challenges, the gifts and miracles—*we did good*."

The Sanctity of Family

To raise an aging parent is to be a good son or daughter. This includes helping the parent through life's passages and its ending. If we have also had the experience of becoming a parent, we know the many joys and challenges of raising a child. But raising a child or taking care of an aging parent is, most of all, a matter of loving and elevating them.

Leaving a Legacy of Love: Creating the Best Possible Future

As we raise them to new heights, we also grow into greater versions of ourselves. Being a parent brings out the best in us as human beings. We are able to love, give to, sacrifice for, serve, and support another person significantly more than we were able to in the past. Raising an aging parent allows our relationship with our parents to grow into its highest expression and flourish.

As small children, we loved our parents with a kind of dependent innocence. As we grew up, our love may have deepened or been diminished by disappointment, despair, or flaws in the way we were raised. As adults, we all have a choice. We can remain bitter and blame our parents for everything that goes wrong in our lives, or we can learn to embrace all the imperfections and resolve that our parents did the best they could with what they had. While it may not always be possible to cultivate a heart of gratitude rather than resentment, we can practice forgiveness and make peace with our parents. By doing so, and breaking the cycle of parent-generated pain, we create a new and improved template for the next generations.

Some of our world's greatest and most inspiring leaders suffered terrible familial adversity, endured unspeakable injustices, and grew up in impoverished, war-torn communities. But these men and women summoned the strength to raise us all up by turning their deepest wounds into a healing, guiding, and enduring standard.

A family that aspires to peace and leaves a legacy of love for the next generation is a gift to its members and to its friends, neighbors, community, and cultures. A family in which members treat one another with love and respect is a beacon to all of us. As all of us work hard to make our families better and stronger, we are also making our communities better and stronger.

Raising aging parents with a loving heart, helping them put their houses in order, holding their hands through difficult transitions, allowing ourselves to be loved and appreciated, taking good care of ourselves as caregivers, and keeping our families strong through good, sound communication defines us as good sons and daughters and represents a gift to our children, grandchildren, and others we may not even know in the world we share. There is no better way to show eternal gratitude for the life you have been given than to pay the good forward, leaving a legacy of love.

Before I go, I want to thank you for going on this journey with me. It is my hope that you are better able to open up a constructive, caring, and supportive dialogue with your parents, siblings and members of your "chosen" family as the result of reading this book and doing the exercises. Making peace with our parents, siblings and beloved members of our chosen families in this lifetime may not be easy, but it's worth the effort. May every joy, blessing and moment of peace be yours, Ken.

You can find out more information on the paperback, hardcover, & audio versions of this book on www.KenDruck.com and www.Amazon.com. *The Raising an Aging Parent Journal* is a companion workbook for readers who want to delve deeper into the issues and opportunities featured in this book. To learn more or purchase a copy, please go to www.kendruck.com.

Dr. Ken Druck is available as a speaker, coach, consultant, workshop/meeting facilitator, retreat leader or for media interviews, by emailing info@kendruck.com or calling the offices of Druck Enterprises Inc. in Del Mar, California at (858) 863-7825.

Acknowledgments

Books don't just happen. They are nothing less than business start ups with a team of talented and dedicated professionals, loyal friends and ardent supporters. This book would not be in your hands today were it not for my incomparable publisher, Sara Stratton of Redwood Publishing, my editor-turned-friend-turned- brother, Michael Levin, my world class publicity team at Wasabi Publicity, my *Raising an Aging Parent* brilliant campaign team at Druck Enterprises Inc., Mary Marcdante and Melanie Merritt, my dear friends, Arielle Ford, John Assaraf, Mike Koenigs, Ken Key, Stewart and Joanie Emery, my partners-in-good at The Oasis Institute (Simona, Jolyn and Paul), my brilliant audio book producer/composer, Mark Spiro, my beloved family, daughter, Stefie, son-in-law and editor, Tony, twin grandsons, Stone and Andrix and my beloved life-partner, Lisette, who supported, inspired and shared her sage wisdom and breadth of experience with me daily (and then took this beautiful cover photo of my, my daughter's and my grandson's hands). To all of you, my heartfelt and eternal gratitude.